# TOWER OF THE HAND

# OTHER BOOKS WRITTEN
# BY THE EDITOR

It Is Known: An Analysis of Thrones, Vol. I
(*Game of Thrones*, season one)

It Is Known: An Analysis of Thrones, Vol. II
(*Game of Thrones*, season two)

Green Switch Palace:
A Year in the Life of Nintendo Fandom

# OTHER BOOKS PUBLISHED
# BY BLUE BUDDHA PRESS

It Is Known: Season 3 Deconstructed
*by Stefan Sasse*

Waiting for Winter: Re-Reading *A Clash of Kings*
*by Remy Verhoeve*

# TOWER OF THE HAND: A FLIGHT OF SORROWS

## COLLECTOR'S EDITION

### EDITED BY

### MARC N. KLEINHENZ

# COPYRIGHT ACKNOWLEDGEMENTS

Cover Design by Josh Esenwine

Cover Photograph by Carrie Butcher-Kleinhenz

Special thanks to Don Zalewski

BLUE BUDDHA PRESS

First edition

ISBN: 978-0615890005

# Contents

## REGULAR EDITION

# Contents

## COLLECTOR'S EDITION

*For Brock*

REGULAR EDITION

# FOREWORD

*And Now It Begins...*

Let me take you back, all the way back, to those heady days of 2003. I was in college. I had always been a reader and usually gravitated towards science fiction and fantasy. I had already read *The Lord of the Rings* and *The Wheel of Time*, so my friend loaned me this book, which he said was good and that I should read it. I don't remember him giving me any details about it. The book was called *A Game of Thrones*.

It looked like any other fantasy novel. Guy on horseback, check. White wolf at his side, check. Castle in the background, check. I started reading it, got a few chapters in, and... stopped. It didn't really grab me right off the bat. (Come to find out, this is a common reaction.) A year or so goes by, and I get a new job, a nighttime security job, in which I find myself with a lot of empty hours. So I decide to give the book another go.

This time, I read it, and I get sucked in. I devour all of *Game*, blaze through *A Clash of Kings*, and then ride out the twists and turns of *A Storm of Swords*. I couldn't get enough. These were easily the best books I had ever read. The thing about *A Song of Ice and Fire* is it's not a series that one just reads and then goes, "Well, that was good. What should I read next?" No, it stays with you. You go over and over it in your head. This is a series that warrants deeper analysis and discussion.

So I did what any self-respecting college student would do – I turned to the internet. And that's when a whole new world was opened up to me. There were dozens of websites out there, with thousands of people participating in discussions over the many mysteries within the *Ice and Fire* series. Right away, I discovered a site that would become one of my go-to destinations: Tower of the Hand. Their detailed chapter summaries and extensive glossary were reason enough to keep coming back to the site, but they added to that thought-provoking and deep analysis of the series and research into its central mysteries. Who is Azor Ahai reborn? Who are Jon Snow's parents? Are Renly and Loras gay? All the major questions that anyone reading the series through for the first time would ask themselves (and some they may not think to ask) were dissected and weighed and discussed.

I think most people would agree that those early days of discovery are some of the best times in *Ice and Fire* fandom. These books are so deep that you don't even realize how many hints and clues and deeper themes you may have missed on your first read-through. Discovering all that is very exciting and heightens your appreciation and passion for the series.

This collection of essays looks to bring back those days. So whether you are a longtime fan of the series who's been here since the beginning, or whether you just got into the books recently due to the HBO series, you should find something here that is new to you – something that will bring back that sense of discovery.

The authors here, many of whom are behind Tower of the Hand and their excellent analysis, have come up with some topics relevant to the current state of *Song of Ice and Fire* fandom. They have dug deep to find the deeper meanings and hidden answers that are always present in George R.R. Martin's work.

So allow this book to take you back, back to those early days, when new discoveries and new answers awaited you around every corner, when the mysteries were still mysterious and the hidden themes still eluded you. Allow this book to rekindle that new fan feeling.

I know it will for me.


*Phil Bicking*
*Editor and Creator of*
*WinterIsComing.net*

# INTRODUCTION

*All along the Watchtower*

Marc N. Kleinhenz

One of A Podcast of Ice and Fire's (more sane) traditions is to ask all new guests on their show how they first got into George R.R. Martin's terrifyingly immersive *A Song of Ice and Fire* series. To honor the podcast hosts' graciousness in joining us Tower of the Handers in this rather experimental undertaking, I figured I would keep up the tradition. (All resultant levels of boredom can, thus, be laid safely and exclusively at their feet. Tell them Marc sent you.)

The fall of 2006 saw me and my wife living in Kobe, Japan, as English teachers for a private corporation. It was, on the whole, a rather rewarding experience, though the company was easily among the worst either one of us had ever had the misfortune of working for (literally a month or two after we made it back home Stateside, it went belly-up and left all several hundred of its *gaijin* employees stranded in apartments that they suddenly couldn't pay for, cementing its status as a Shitty Company). Facing a two-train, 45-minute commute to and from the office each and every day (I worked at the Diamond City shopping mall in tiny Itami, just 10 minutes west of Osaka), and stranded in a country where I could speak my native tongue only slowly and haltingly, I devoured books like I haven't before or since; my typical rate of reading one book a month easily tripled, and I even managed to go beyond my usual purview of nonfiction, research-related reading to that marvelous and mysterious thing called literature.    It was pleasant.

It was also exciting.    For some strange reason, I found myself latching on to the reading habits of a co-worker from Michigan; whatever he read, I would ultimately read, going from Henry Kissinger's *Diplomacy* (which was mainly responsible for my current obsession with politics, generally, and presidential history, specifically) to this obviously hackneyed fantasy tripe with an absolutely awful title called *A Game of Thrones*. I easily spent the first two-thirds of the novel complaining of the obvious and clumsy worldbuilding, the blatant impinging of Tolkien (the "children of the forest"? Civilizations sailing across the Sea? *Please*), and the steady misuse of the comma.    By the time it ended and I was clamoring to pick up the next book, and the one after and the one after, I knew I was hopelessly, mercilessly hooked and that Martin was, indeed, a writer of incredible ability (punctuational mechanics aside, of course).    I have never looked back since.

Actually, that's an understatement.    My obsessive-compulsive tendencies kicked in on a regular and then on an exponential basis, making me evaluate, analyze, and deconstruct Martin's rather convoluted narrative in constant fits and starts, much to the chagrin of my poor wife, who had to hear such meandering soliloquies all the way from Japan to America (and the 13-hour flight in-between), not to mention all throughout the five years since.    She had the rather polite request of rerouting all my energies to an appropriate outlet, which, since the time of our Asian sojourn, was increasingly freelance journalism. When I ended up quitting my post as features editor for TotalPlayStation.com (a wonderful site run by the even more wonderful Sam Bishop, alumnus of IGN's Podcast Beyond [the show is irreparably diminished without him and my other cohort-of-sorts, Chris Roper] and purveyor of the Great Laugh) in April 2011, the opportunity finally arose to do just that.

Given the sheer amount of time that helming features took at TPS, I figured that I'd be able to write for three new sites just once or twice a month and *still* be ahead of the time deficit game (I was right). The following month, my first article for ToweroftheHand.com was up. Two months later, my book-by-book series of essays was temporarily scrapped – no, it still hasn't been completed to this day, thank you for asking – but my monthly contributions were continued. I was a bona fide TOTH regular, whether Johnny or Alex, the site's two superb founders, liked it or not.

Tower of the Hand is, of course, an invaluable resource in the ever-expanding *Ice and Fire* universe, and in addition to assisting the real heavy-lifters at the site, such as Miles or the incomparable Stefan, my role quickly shaped up to be a self-imposed attempt at ever expanding the site's offerings. In short order, I conducted TOTH's first audio interview (with Ted Nasmith, one of the nicest – and most talented – chaps you'll ever meet this side of the border), spoke with Amin and Mimi about their delightfully dysfunctional podcast, and instituted a monthly intra-site roundtable – but it wasn't enough. My efforts at pushing and antagonizing weren't sated until we all hit on the idea of doing this standalone ebook publication.

Amazingly enough, Johnny and Alex were game every step of the primrose way, the poor bastards, even in handing the editorial reins over to me for this project. (The story of how *A Flight of Sorrows* came to be – including the sordid evolution of its size, intent, and even lineup – is a story for another time. Suffice to say it involved blackmail. And pliers.) And now you're holding it in your hands.

But what to expect? As all of us have not made a secret of, we felt there was something of a gaping hole in the contextual landscape surrounding *A Song of Ice and Fire*: professional analysis without the literati detritus that tends to clog such endeavors (I'm looking at you, my poor *The Matrix and Philosophy*). We wanted investigations about the story, and not about the literary aspects *around* the story. Or explorations of characterization and plot developments and thematic motifs, and not surveys of critical reactions to said narrative handiwork. We wanted, in other words, what readers have not only come to expect, but also to rely upon, for the past seven years at Tower of the Hand. And that we've been able to undertake such a journey with members from all across the spectrum of *Ice and Fire* fandom – from A Podcast of Ice and Fire to WinterIsComing.net to, I think, the most enjoyable site of them all, InnattheCrossroads.com – only makes it that much sweeter (no pun intended).

Actually, a journey is a good analogy to employ; much like Tyrion making his way slowly down the Rhoyne, floating through the Sorrows and all its attendant dangers, we authors have attempted to delve directly into Martin's thematic heart. Prophecies of smoke and salt, assassinations and murders, marital infidelity and adultery – all are sorrows, aflight.

And we thank you for riding the narrative winds with us.

# WARNING

The essays in this anthology analyze significant events from all five books that comprise *A Song of Ice and Fire* to date. Please read only if you're caught up or if you don't mind learning disturbing details about the remainder of the story.

# UNDER THE BLEEDING STAR

*On the role of prophecy in songs of ice and fire*

Stefan Sasse

*"You wear your prophecy like a suit of armor. You think it keeps you safe, but all it does is weigh you down and make it hard for you to move."*

Littlefinger (paraphrased)

If there is one topic that really engages fan speculation, it's the subject of prophecies. They can be found in the books as early as *A Game of Thrones*, when the Dothraki *dosh khaleen* prophesizes the arrival of "The Stallion Who Mounts the World" in the incarnation of Daenerys Targaryen's son, Rhaego, and they stay with us until the long-awaited pages of *A Dance with Dragons*, where Quaithe makes another appearance and a red priest named Moqorro utters dark phrases to anyone who listens. One of the most memorable scenes of Dany's whole character arc, the House of the Undying, is littered with prophecy.

For the reader, who has a better look at the whole picture than the individual protagonists do, trying to decipher these very metaphorical prophecies has become a fun game, and trying to figure out which prophecies have already been fulfilled is yet another source of never-ending entertainment. In fact, so many have done this so well, this can hardly be the place to discuss, yet again, who will be the "head of the dragon," which mounts Dany has to ride, and who, exactly, is Azor Ahai reborn. Instead, we will take a deeper look at what the prophecies mean for the people in Westeros and Essos themselves. How do they react to prophecy, what do they make of it, and what role does it play in their actual lives?

Both sides of the narrow sea have to be regarded as lands that are ruled by elites who disdain superstition, or what they think of as superstition. The infamous grumkins and snarks are often used as stand-ins for such things – whoever believes in any magical stuff probably believes in these and other children's stories, too, and is, therefore, not to be taken seriously. Much of this must be attributed to the maesters of the Citadel. They are learned men, wise in what can be viewed as sort-of medieval science, and they are utterly opposed to anything magical. They counsel every important lord and his progeny, and, thus, their views on the world have tremendous impact on the mindset of the Westerosi nobility. The prevailing attitude has long been one that is poised against such ideas as dreams coming true, obsidian candles burning, or dragons roaming the skies again.

In Essos, the elite are constituted a little bit more on wealth and merit, but this is still no landscape that affords superstition; where numbers, coins, and balance books comprise everything you are and do, there is no room for magical stories. In Essos, as well as in Westeros, magic and prophecy are the domain of the religious, of children, and, of course, of the lower classes – those social realms ignorant enough to believe in such things. It is no wonder that the religion with the greatest amount of "magic stuff," the cult of R'hllor, is, at its heart, a poor man's faith. The tired, poor, huddled masses flock to the nightfires, while the elites revel in their more aristocratic beliefs, if they have any at all. It is really hard to imagine people like Illyrio Mopatis giving even a second glance at the idea of a "Prince That Was Promised" or a "Mummer's Dragon." Things either work or they don't.

> *"When the red star bleeds and the darkness gathers, Azor Ahai shall be born again amidst smoke and salt."*
>
> Melisandre of Asshai

Therefore, one of the big remaining mysteries is how a man like Stannis Baratheon, so deeply rooted in the idea of a mundane world, where laws are made and obeyed by men, winds up with a woman like Melisandre of Asshai. Initially, his relationship with her is purely utilitarian; she has her uses, which may or may not be magical. It's not until the Battle of the Blackwater that he becomes a true believer, when he finally, grudgingly acknowledges Melisandre's superior skills in an art he cannot understand and doesn't really bother to try. He becomes entrenched in it, applying his sense of duty not only to the role of king, but now also to Azor. Most likely, he sees it as another burden he must carry by birth and station (Stannis Baratheon is *never* one to embrace religious fervor, unlike Lancel Lannister).

And he doesn't hesitate to go all the way. Once he decides to believe Melisandre (again, we don't know why and how this comes to pass), he commands the burning of the old gods, takes up a new sigil, and forces his bannermen to do likewise. At the heart of this religious conversion and the ensuing war that more and more looks like a jihad is the prophecy of Azor Ahai, brought to the reader (and Davos Seaworth) by courtesy of Salladhor Saan. From him, we learn that Azor Ahai, the hero of heroes, could only forge his magical sword Lightbringer by sacrificing what he loved most, his wife, Nissa Nissa.

So, if Stannis is Azor reincarnated and truly believes in this prophecy, what does he sacrifice? When he gains his Lightbringer, which is called false by Maester Aemon (not a man whose testimony is to be taken lightly), he burns the Seven, a faith he surely never loved. In fact, Stannis Baratheon doesn't love – not his wife and child, not the throne he wants to conquer, not the god he has taken, not the red woman he beds. Sacrifice comes naturally to him. He has no problem sacrificing people, because he sacrifices so much of himself in the name of duty; his honor and his dignity have already gone to waste during Robert's time, and the only thing left to him, his sense of justice, perished at Storm's End with the death of Renly.

If Stannis believes in being Azor Ahai – another thing we can't entirely be sure of – then even more suffering will ensue. A Stannis Baratheon who believes that he is the rightful heir and that it is his duty to ascend to the throne, even if he doesn't want to, is a man who will literally stop at nothing if he is also pumped up with religious fervor over being the chosen one. The image of him brooding atop his lonely tower in *A Dance with Dragons*, staring out into the whirling snows and only emerging to silently watch some offenders burn in the glory of R'hllor is a vivid image of what type of king this man would make. It is like Littlefinger's prophecy (no pun intended) to Lord Eddard Stark: Stannis would

mean war and suffering.  A man so determined
that he would suffer through the Northern winter
just to fight a war that, by all accounts, looks to
be futile is not a man you want to believe in being
destined by god to sit the Iron Throne.

Yet the prophecy did not come to Stannis
by chance.  It was brought by a woman with a
mission, one not really sanctioned by her religious
institution.  Melisandre of Asshai is convinced that
she knows who has to be Azor Ahai, and that it is
her duty to help him awaken to his path.  In the
way she kickstarts events, she mirrors Littlefinger
– she's on the sidelines, whispering in the ear of a
mighty lord, setting him in motion.  Her belief, we
now know (thanks to *Dance with Dragons*), is
genuine.   She is, however, a political power
player.  She isn't shy of using her credibility as a
prophet to steer people.  Her burning of leeches is
a prime example of this; she saw the deaths of
Renly Baratheon, Robb Stark, and Balon Greyjoy in
the flames and makes a spectacle of it to leverage
Stannis to give her what she wants.  She needs to
build up credibility like this desperately – she's
not only a foreigner, preaching of a foreign god,
she also proclaims a prophecy nobody basically
ever heard of, and she does so to convince others
to start a war based on it.  (Of course, the
problem with all this is that she's wrong; she
clearly misreads visions without even knowing it
and commits all to suffering based on the simple
vanity of wanting to be a seer.)

Although the prophecy of Azor Ahai is a
cornerstone of Westeros, circa 299 AL, only a
small number of people seem to really know about
it, and most of these are Stannis's bannermen.  It
is interesting that the prophecy never came up in
a meeting of the small council; at some point, the
information of Stannis's beliefs must have found
its way to King's Landing, but somehow nobody

thought it noteworthy that the contender they had long regarded as the most dangerous had converted to a religion that regarded him as the messiah. Religion is nothing taken too seriously in the nobility of the southron kingdoms, obviously. But without it, it may be that Stannis might never have sailed. Certainly, he would have had no means of defeating Renly. Without Melisandre's interference, fueled by the burning fire of a prophecy fulfilled, Westeros would be a different place. This impact cannot be taken lightly.

This becomes even truer if we look back 19 years. Rhaegar Targaryen also believed in a prophecy: the Prince That Was Promised. There is much debate about whether this legendary prince is identical with Azor Ahai or not, but the truth is we don't know much about the actual prophecy (and, either way, this is not the place for that particular discussion). What is most important about it is in its influence on how events have unfolded. As a boy, Rhaegar read something in a scroll – the prediction of the prince, most likely – and decided that it was time for him to become a warrior. Though he did have some talent in this regard, he was never Aemon the Dragonknight reborn, and he later changed his mind, anyway, and assigned the role of the foretold prince to his son, Aegon. He still saw it as his duty to set things in motion to fulfill legend, though; like Melisandre (and, to a lesser extent, Stannis), he saw it as his personal responsibility to do what fate ordered him to do.

It is not known what reasoning went into his actions, but it surely informed his decision to abscond with Lyanna Stark. Religiosity, then, was a direct cause of the War of the Usurper, the downfall of House Targaryen, and the deaths of Rhaegar and his fabled son, whose head was famously dashed against the wall. Robert's

Rebellion can't be imagined without Rhaegar's actions, igniting the fuse that led to the murders of Rickard and Brandon Stark and also to King Aerys's demand to Jon Arryn.

The Prince That Was Promised and Azor Ahai are at least similar in their scope of impact. Both foretell the arrival of a messiah to battle an important, mighty enemy afflicted with coldness and darkness and averse to fire and light. In Azor Ahai's case, the prophecy is bound to the faith of R'hllor, while the Prince That Was Promised seems more like a Targaryen-exclusive item, but both feature the same inescapable outcome:  the two major wars of the last twenty years, Robert's Rebellion and the War of the Five Kings, have been defined largely by odd and widely unknown prophecies that were enacted by key players who believed in them. It was not important that they convinced others; Rhaegar as well as Stannis act on their own terms, standing above the petty interests of their underlings. And both are ill-advised to do so.

This is hardly an exclusive attribute to either them or their kind of prophecy, however. Besides Melisandre, the double novel that is *A Feast for Crows* and *A Dance with Dragons* also brings us another prophet, even called that in one of his POV chapters:  Aeron Damphair. The Greyjoy priest is a more ambiguous figure in terms of championing a real prophecy, but that is known only to the reader. He himself believes that he can hear the Drowned God in the crashing of waves, and an ever-growing number of followers believes so, too.  On the Iron Islands, the Damphair is a respected figure because of his relentless conviction.  He doesn't articulate a clear prophecy like Melisandre does, for sure, and he oftentimes covers up insecurities with thunderous-but-empty phrases, but he nonetheless is a prophet, in the sense of being a mouthpiece of his god, if not in delivering predictions to his people.

That he does speak with divine authority is most evident when he declares that "no godless man will sit the Seastone Chair" and calls for a kingsmoot. He prophesizes that the Drowned God will make his will known on Old Wyk, choose a new king for them (which is, undoubtedly, Victarion Greyjoy), and lead the Iron Men into a new iron age. Of course, Aeron doesn't really know what will happen on Old Wyk – he inadvertently sets events in motion that lead to Euron Crow's Eye's ascension to the throne. The takeaway here is that, once again, prophecy has shaped the destinies of entire peoples.

> *"The old gods stir and will not let me sleep. I dreamt I saw a shadow with a burning heart butchering a golden stag, aye. I dreamt of a man without a face, waiting on a bridge that swayed and swung. On his shoulder perched a drowned crow with seaweed hanging from his wings. I dreamt of a roaring river and a woman that was a fish. Dead she drifted, with red tears on her cheeks, but when her eyes did open, oh, I woke from terror."*

> The Ghost of High Heart

The Ghost of High Heart is acting on a much smaller scale, at least today. She dreams of things coming true, although in very metaphorical ways, and sells the knowledge, along with some sketchy interpretations, if she has some and is in the mood for it. We see her giving information to the brotherhood without banners, and Thoros of Myr and Beric Dondarrion seem to have more experience with her and a better understanding than we as readers do, since her dreams are fairly cryptic if one doesn't already know of the events they describe.   It's not entirely clear to what extent Beric and Thoros use the Ghost as a source of intelligence, but they certainly go through the trouble of seeking her out.  This makes it safe to assume that they put some weight into her pronouncements, and it also means that the brotherhood acts on predictions and visions, delivered by a prophet of (presumably) the old gods.

That she is an agent of the children of the forest's deities is a detail that the characters themselves can't possibly know and only we as readers can deduct.  In *Dance*, Ser Barristan Selmy delivers this information almost casually to Dany, indicating that the Ghost not only belongs to the old gods, but also that she is responsible for the marriage between Aerys II and Rhaella Targaryen, and that she came to court with Jenny of Oldstones, who was the love of Duncan the Small, Prince of Dragonflies (and the firstborn son of Aegon V, of the Tales of Dunk and Egg fame).  This strikes the connection to Rhaegar, since the Ghost of High Heart (referred to as the "woods witch" by Barristan) knew about the Prince That Was Promised and told the Targaryens that he would be born of the line of Aerys and Rhaella.  Given that Aerys didn't exactly seem the type for prophecies – unlike Aegon V, Duncan, and Prince Duncan's lover, Jenny of Oldstones – it's likely that most knowledge of that connection was destroyed in the burning of Summerhall the night of Egg's death.  It's also likely that Rhaegar's morbid fascination with the ruins stems from his discovery of the legend in the ancient scrolls.  In this way, the old prophecy binds together the story threads and sets the actors in motion.

> *"When will I marry the prince?"*
>
> *"Never. You will wed the king."*
>
> *"I will be queen, though?"*
>
> *"Aye. Queen you shall be... until there comes another, younger and more beautiful, to cast you down and take all that you hold dear."*
>
> *"Will the king and I have children?"*
>
> *"Oh, aye. Six-and-ten for him, three for you. Gold shall be their crowns and gold their shrouds. And when your tears have drowned you, the* valonqar *shall wrap his hands around your pale white throat and choke the life from you."*
>
> Cersei and Maggy the Frog

This prophecy is one of the most important in the whole saga, and there is only one person who knows about it: Cersei Lannister. (The other eyewitness, Melara Hetherspoon, is disposed of by Cersei, by being thrown down a well.)

The case of Maggy's prophecy is really interesting. Not only do we learn that she is a maegi (the sound of that word should raise some uncomfortable feelings, after *A Game of Thrones*), she also is most likely the woman that old Lord Westerling married. This creepy coincidence aside, Maggy's prediction is responsible for almost everything that happens in the King's Landing storyline in *Feast for Crows*. Cersei is convinced not only that she is reading the prophecy correctly, but that she also is able to forestall and eventually evade it. And she has every reason to believe so: everything Maggy prophesized came true, except, of course, for the last part, which is still to happen. Cersei has a rather broad base of information from which to judge and interpret the prophecy.

She still gets it totally wrong, however. It seems very likely that Margaery Tyrell isn't the younger queen to take everything away from her – that would be Daenerys. It seems likely Tyrion isn't the *valonqar* – that would be Jaime Lannister. Cersei can't know this, and she has literally no chance *of* knowing this. In her desire to prevent the final, fatal part of the prediction from happening, she takes such actions as to bring about her own demise; the Tyrells would never have acquired the position of power they have now if Cersei wouldn't have attempted to put Margaery on trial.

> *"As swift as the wind he rides, and behind him his* khalasar *covers the Earth, men without number, with* arakhs *shining in their hands like blades of razor grass. Fierce as a storm this prince will be. His enemies will tremble before him, and their wives will weep tears of blood and rend their flesh in grief. The bells in his hair will sing his coming, and the milk men in the stone tents will fear his name. The prince is riding, and he shall be the stallion who mounts the world."*

> The *dosh khaleen*

No character in the whole series is as conscious about prophecies as Daenerys Targaryen or is as guided by them. She encounters prophecy early on, and, unlike Stannis or Rhaegar, she does so in an environment that is open to them. It's in the Dothraki capital, Vaes Dothrak, where the *dosh khaleen* – the old wise women of the tribes, whose job it is to head the Dothraki nation, such as it is – prophesize that her son would be the "Stallion Who Mounts the World," which can be seen as yet another variation of the Prince That Was Promised or Azor Ahai. Yet this very early prophecy does not come to pass (at least, not as the crones interpreted it; there's always room for metaphorical explanations), as Dany's son, Rhaego, died in her womb. And even the Dothraki themselves, although conscious of the prophecy, don't seem to hold it in too high regard: they are not above slaying Dany and her child in order to consolidate their own power.

In fact, it's strange that the role of this Stallion is never quite clear in the books – the prophecy falters too fast. In the narrative, it seems to serve the function of discrediting the concept of prophecy itself. It's the first we hear in the series, and it is contradicted before we ever learn another (Bran's dreams excluded).

Shortly after Rhaego's death, Dany hears her next prediction: only when the sun sets in the east and rises in the west, when the mountains blow in the wind like leaves, and when the sea goes dry, will she bear a living child and have Khal Drogo return to her. When Mirri Maz Duur spits these words in Dany's face, she doesn't take them as a prophecy, but thinks it just means "never." It is not entirely clear what Mirri Maz Duur's intent was. Was she aware she was making a prophecy, or is it mere coincidence? At the end of *Dance*, no one can be sure anymore. Dany's womb seems to have quickened again, Quentyn Martell (who has the sun in his arms and comes from the west to die in the east) has perished, a pyramid was reduced to ashes whirling in the wind, and a dragon named Drogon, who was thought lost, returned. Dany hasn't jumped to that conclusion yet, but in a narrative function, it works again to unsettle the reader and plant the seed of doubt.

> *"To go north, you must go south. To reach the west, you must go east. To go forward, you must go back, and to touch the light, you must pass beneath the shadow."*

> Qaithe

Dany is a person driven by a sense of fate, anyway. Even if she doesn't accept Mirri Maz Duur's words as prophecy, there is an aura of determination surrounding her. She acts as if she were destined to do whatever she is doing at the moment, an attitude that certainly was strongly encouraged over the course of *A Clash of Kings* and *A Storm of Swords*.

Let's recap for a moment. First she breeds the first living dragons in two centuries, then she survives the Red Waste, defeats the Undying, conquers Astapor, defeats the Yunkish army, and storms Mereen. There, of course, it starts to fall to pieces, but what a ride it has been! Imagine her taking the demon road and conquering Volantis, freeing the largest slave population in the world – it would have cemented her image. The road she took after she defeated the Undying was already pregnant with the air of prophecy. When they told her "Three fires must you light... one for life and one for death and one to love... three mounts must you ride... one to bed and one to dread and one to love... three treasons will you know... once for blood and once for gold and once for love," she took it to heart. She's constantly wondering whether the prophecy has already been fulfilled or not. Her decisions are impacted greatly by her fears of its wording – who might be the next betrayer? She believes she can't avoid the prediction, but perhaps she can take away some of its impact.

At this point, the question of free will forces itself into the picture once again, since there's no certainty about whether the prophecy *must* come true or not. But before we can ruminate on this point in full, we need to first look at the last kind of prophecy in the books we haven't covered yet: greenseeing.

> *He saw his mother sitting alone in a cabin, looking at a bloodstained knife on a table in front of her, as the rowers pulled at their oars and Ser Rodrik leaned across a rail, shaking and heaving. A storm was gathering ahead of them, a vast dark roaring lashed by lightning, but somehow they could not see it.*

> *He saw his father pleading with the king, his face etched with grief. He saw Sansa crying herself to sleep at night, and he saw Arya watching in silence and holding her secrets hard in her heart. There were shadows all around them. One shadow was as dark as ash, with the terrible face of a hound. Another was armored like the sun, golden and beautiful. Over them both loomed a giant in armor made of stone, but when he opened his visor, there was nothing inside but darkness and thick black blood.*

*He lifted his eyes and saw clear across the narrow sea, to the Free Cities and the green Dothraki sea and beyond, to Vaes Dothrak under its mountain, to the fabled lands of the Jade Sea, to Asshai by the Shadow, where dragons stirred beneath the sunrise.*

*Finally, he looked north. He saw the Wall shining like blue crystal, and his bastard brother Jon sleeping alone in a cold bed, his skin growing pale and hard as the memory of all warmth fled from him.*

*North and north and north he looked, to the curtain of light at the end of the world, and then beyond that curtain. He looked deep into the heart of winter, and then he cried out, afraid, and the heat of his tears burned his cheeks.*

Now you know, *the crow whispered as it sat on his shoulder.* Now you know why you must live.

*"Why?" Bran said, not understanding, falling, falling.*

Because winter is coming.

*Bran looked down. There was nothing below him now but snow and cold and death, a frozen wasteland where jagged blue-white spires of ice waited to embrace him. They flew up at him like spears. He saw the bones of a thousand other dreamers impaled upon their points.   He was desperately afraid.*

Bran's dream

Bran's prophecies are perhaps the most interesting and beautifully haunting ones, at least for me.  He truly looks behind the curtain of his mortal existence and crosses the boundaries of mundane materiality.   He also doesn't try to interpret what he sees, at least not until *A Dance with Dragons*.  He's communicating more or less directly with the forces (which we now know to mainly be Lord Bloodraven, from the Tales of Dunk and Egg) that actually make the prophecies. This is an interesting diversion from other characters dealing with predictions, whether they actively seek them out or are handed them by other agents.

One could make an argument about whether what Bran sees are really prophecies.  In the end, the three-eyed crow is just Bloodraven inviting him into the Far North, where Bran eventually arrives in his second chapter of *Dance*. It is not yet entirely clear why the message was so cryptic.   Is it because Bloodraven is no longer really connected to the hearts and minds of average people anymore?  Is it because the magic of the greenseers doesn't allow for any type of clear communication?   Or does he just want to pique Bran's curiosity?  Whatever it is, obviously it is not enough to get a seven-year-old boy on such a journey.   Luckily, we have Jojen Reed, who is also highly susceptible to such things.

Looking through the ages using weirwoods seems to be more a kind of magic than an act of the old gods or prophecy (a point I made at length in my essay about the true origins of religion, which    can    still    be    checked    out    at

ToweroftheHand.com).     Bran's prophecies, therefore, really qualify as a matter of communication, as do Jojen Reed's.   What they receive are almost exclusively warnings, encrypted in metaphor, but clear enough to those who can read them.   Jojen is really good at this sort of thing, but like Melisandre, he can't get the logic of a warning if he lacks sufficient information (the sea coming to Winterfell in Jojen's case;   the towers of Eastwatch in Melisandre's).   Unlike Melisandre, however, Jojen is humble enough not to jump to conclusions just for the sake of grandstanding.

Having explored the prophecies as they appear in the story, there are still three unanswered questions left to deal with.   The first is whether or not there is a special purpose of or to these prophecies.   (If so, this would imply that an external force is broadcasting them, and only those with a sensitive enough antenna can receive them.)   Second, is there such a thing as free will in a world where the future is so obviously predetermined (knowing it doesn't change it, as Stannis painfully learns on the Blackwater)?   And third, what consequences does the existence of prophecy have for Westerosi society?

First questions first.   It seems like the "true" prophecies we have experienced – the ones that are fairly clear (Aeron Greyjoy's over-interpretation of the sound of waves doesn't qualify) – contain accurate descriptions of the future.   Daenerys gets some (the vaguest ones, too), as do the greenseers Bran and Jojen and the followers of R'hllor, Moqorro, Thoros, and Melisandre.   Of the latter, Melisandre seems to be seeing things for the longest duration of time, having sought out Stannis before the Red Comet arrived, while Moqorro and Thoros started their visions only when the comet appeared and the dragons were born.  In the case of Bloodraven, he uses greenseeing to perfection and knows about the threat of the Others.  Bran seems to play some role in the grand scheme of things and needs to help him, so he uses glimpses of his knowledge to lure Bran into the North (by way of Jojen).

Daenerys, however, gets prophecies from various sources.  Nonetheless, they seem to come true, and they, too, seem to come in the disguise of warnings most of the time.  Melisandre and her ilk also use the visions of the flames to avoid lurking dangers, as we learn from her own chapter in *Dance with Dragons*, so it seems fair to conclude that, in most cases, prophecies serve to warn their recipients.  They also seem to be effective when used in one other, more profane way:  as information, as we see with the brotherhood without banners utilizing Thoros as well as the Ghost of High Heart as a kind of medieval CNN or GPS device.

These deliberations bring us to question number two.  If prophecies serve as warnings, then is there free will?  Despite knowing the future, events still transpire as predicted in every single case, even if the various actors were able to read the prophecies correctly.  Distilled down to their bare essence like this, it seems almost hilarious how frequently the predictions are misjudged due to missing information – which then causes the recipients to inadvertently fulfill them.  Indeed, the self-fulfilling prophecy surely is a topic not unknown to George R.R. Martin.  In fact, we have no situation (yet) in the books where a character gets a prophecy and immediately deduces its meaning correctly.  Even more to the point, there is never a situation like this even for the reader, with his supreme advantage of having access to the entire story.

Unsatisfying as it may be, we simply can't say whether there is free will or not. Until now, all that has happened could have been a pure product of chance. The players are acting with incomplete information, and they can never be sure of their interpretations; since they can't do anything else, they have to make do with their limited knowledge and experience, which leads to interpretative errors like the ones Melisandre produces with alarming regularity. It's only mumbo-jumbo like the business with the leeches that helps her to retain her position as Stannis's most trusted advisor.

Then there's the smallfolk. Interestingly enough, prophecies seem to be more a thing of the learned people, despite their unwillingness to discuss them publicly. We know of no prophecies the smallfolk believe in, not even some savior or messiah who will come and make everything right for them at some point in the future, whether that happens to be the Promised Prince or Azor Ahai (two figures which would seem to be especially popular) or not. It is interesting, however, just how much the life of the Westerosi people is influenced by the prophecies; Cersei's actions prove to be consequential for a great number of individuals, but only she knows the rationale behind them. Stannis acts on the "knowledge" of his being the chosen one of the one true god, but he doesn't exactly adapt his marketing strategy to it. And Daenerys has yet to have her beliefs falsified, but she's already conquered two cities, smashed the army of a third, and is in the midst of fighting a rather far-reaching war.

Prophecy is what drives many of the main events of *A Song of Ice and Fire*, but it's not the divine predictions themselves, as if some celestial entity were actively manipulating events (as seen, for example, in the reimagined *Battlestar Galactica*); rather, it's human nature, prone to error and prejudice and ego. This is the essence of what makes prophecies such a compelling narrative theme in the saga: they are not forced unto the reader as they are in many other fantasy stories (such as *Diablo*) – they are instead more a means for the author to communicate with his audience. Prophecies seem to break the fourth wall in a way, as no character (as of yet) has the slightest chance of unraveling the pieces. Only the reader comes close to having the information required.

In the end, however, this could be just another illusion by Martin, who already made his audience believe that Eddard Stark was the central character of his story. We like to believe that we have deciphered a certain prophecy and now know what it means, but if the events of *A Dance with Dragons* – with its highly malleable solutions to such concrete-sounding predictions – are any indication, prophecies are not only a sword without a hilt for the characters, they also are for the readers, as well. For good or for ill, we are bound to interpret and misinterpret them as the characters do themselves and, thus, experience the struggle for knowledge firsthand.

It is known.

# DAGGERS IN THE DARK

*The ultimate fates of protagonists, from* A Game of Thrones *to* A Dance with Dragons

Miles Schneiderman

*He saw the glint of steel, turned toward it. "No* blades!" *he screamed. "Wick, put that knife..."*

*...away, he meant to say.* When Wick Whittlestick slashed at his throat, the word turned into a grunt. Jon twisted from the knife, just enough so it barely grazed his skin. He cut me. When he put his hand to the side of his neck, blood welled between his fingers. "Why?"

*"For the Watch."* Wick slashed at him again. This time, Jon caught his wrist and bent his arm back until he dropped the dagger. The gangling steward backed away, his hands upraised as if to say, Not me, it was not me. Men were screaming. Jon reached for Longclaw, but his fingers had grown stiff and clumsy. Somehow he could not seem to get the sword free of its scabbard.

*Then Bowen Marsh stood there before him, tears running down his cheeks. "For the*

*Watch." He punched Jon in the belly.
When he pulled his hand away, the dagger
stayed where he had buried it.*

*Jon fell to his knees. He found the
dagger's hilt and wrenched it free. In the
cold night air, the wound was smoking.
"Ghost," he whispered. Pain washed over
him. Stick them with the pointy end.
When the third dagger took him between
the shoulder blades, he gave a grunt and
fell face-first into the snow. He never felt
the fourth knife. Only the cold...*

*A Dance with Dragons*, Jon XIII

So ends Jon Snow's final chapter in *A
Dance with Dragons*, and if you believe what
you've just read, so ends his final chapter in *A
Song of Ice and Fire*. It is one of the book's
defining moments and joins an elite pantheon of
horrific events throughout the series, destined to
go down in history alongside Baelor's Sept and the
Red Wedding. Mere days or even hours after the
book's release, millions of fans read the final
words of that chapter and slowly began to realize
that George Martin, the infamous literary slasher,
had done it once again; the most petrifying
persecutor of protagonists since Hamlet
discovered the problem with suicide had claimed
the life of yet another beloved main character.

Jon was dead. We knew that for a fact.
We'd been due, after all. The first book in the
series, *A Game of Thrones*, had featured the
abrupt and now-legendary demise of Lord Eddard
Stark, our presumptive protagonist. Two novels
later, *A Storm of Swords* kept the trend going with
the murder of King Robb Stark and his mother,
Catelyn. And now, in this fifth volume, another of

Ned's sons gets it in the back. Just like his half-brother, Jon Snow was betrayed and stabbed to death by men he believed loyal to him, in a scenario that caught most readers completely off-guard.

The cycle of literary trauma continued. There was only shock at first, and then, almost without thinking about it, there was acceptance. But then, a moment later, there was skepticism – and for good reason.

This is why.

### The Four Arguments

There are four key pieces of evidence that suggest that Jon Snow isn't actually dead, or, at least, that he will have some kind of continued role in the series. Three of these four arguments are situational and should all be part of the same discussion; they are related to the characters involved, the present environment and circumstances of those characters, and a close examination of the words used to describe their thoughts and actions. These situational arguments are as follows:

1. The circumstances of Jon's death as described in the text are rife with odd occurrences and unexplained phenomena, suggesting that readers are not yet privy to what is really going on.

2. Given what we now know of wargs and skinchanging, it is possible that Jon, or some part of him, lives on in Ghost. Therefore, it is also possible that he might somehow be restored.

3.  Jon's death occurred in the immediate vicinity of both Melisandre and the Wall.  Any supernatural properties the latter may possess have not yet been fully defined, but it nonetheless remains a possible influence.  The former, meanwhile, is an extremely powerful practitioner of a religion whose devotees have already demonstrated the ability to bring the dead back to life.

The fourth and final argument involves ideas of narrative structure and established trends in previous writing, as opposed to specifics of the scene.  Here, the contention is that Jon Snow is simply too important a character to have met his demise at the end of only the fifth book.  Those who maintain that this series has already disproved the existence of "plot armor" within its boundaries are allowing a distorted set of facts to combine with a popular misconception, creating the illusion of an absolute truth.  The actual truth is that George Martin is nowhere near the psychotic character-killer that so many believe him to be, and that Jon's status as a main character – and, more importantly, as a point-of-view character – does indeed place him beyond the ranks of those who are allowed to prematurely bite the dust.

We begin, however, with the three in-book reasons why the reports of Jon's death may have been somewhat overstated.  Regardless of potential narrative trends, there are some things happening here that cast doubt on the entire affair.  It's not hard at all to figure out why Jon might not have truly been killed, and, even if he

were, to ascertain the various ways in which he
might come back.

### The Situational Argument: Witches, Wargs, and Weirdness

Let's take another look at that final
passage.  It's not just tragic – there are some
strange things going on.

> *Wick slashed at him again. This time, Jon*
> *caught his wrist and bent his arm back*
> *until he dropped the dagger. The gangling*
> *steward backed away, his hands upraised*
> *as if to say,* Not me, it was not me.

This, for example.  This is odd.  If Jon is
interpreting Wick's hand-raising gesture correctly,
Wick seems to be suddenly avowing his own
innocence.  This makes sense superficially; Wick
has just turned on his lord commander, who then
disarmed him.  He's making a last-ditch effort to
deflect blame, seeing as he finds himself
weaponless against a man he just attacked.

But is this explanation really plausible?
Wick has already slashed at Jon twice.  Why would
he believe for a second that he could beg off
those actions?   And why his sudden lack of
commitment to what must have been a conspiracy
within the Night's Watch to dispose of their
leader?  For that matter, why brazenly declare
your innocence to a person who you know is about
to die?  Why follow up the "for the Watch" line
with a vain act of cowardice?  Something here just
doesn't quite add up.

> *Jon reached for Longclaw, but his fingers*
> *had grown stiff and clumsy.  Somehow he*

*could not seem to get the sword free of its scabbard.*

And what's this about? Was Wick's knife poisoned? Again, it sort of makes sense – the conspirators knew about Jon's fighting skill and might have reasonably wanted a way of slowing him down so they could do him in without any danger of being killed themselves. If that's the case, Wick's act of raising his hands in defense could easily have just been him waiting a few moments for the poison to kick in, though this requires that we discount the "not me, it was not me" description. And in regards to Jon's fingers stiffening up, the fact of the matter is we don't (yet) have a clear explanation – all we have is speculation. Yes, Wick's knife could have been poisoned. Or it could have been something else.

*Jon fell to his knees. He found the dagger's hilt and wrenched it free. In the cold night air, the wound was smoking. "Ghost," he whispered. Pain washed over him. Stick them with the pointy end. When the third dagger took him between the shoulder blades, he gave a grunt and fell face-first into the snow. He never felt the fourth knife. Only the cold...*

Call it a trick of the prose or just really good description, but this entire last paragraph is ambiguous. "The wound was smoking." Is this a poetic way of describing the blood suddenly exposed to the air? Was there blood at all? It's unclear. "Pain washed over him," but it's not localized and it goes almost entirely undescribed. The reference to "stick them with the pointy end" is interesting, and certainly implies that the pointy end of something is on Jon's mind. And then it's quickly made clear that Jon is still getting stabbed – followed, of course, by the final sensation of cold, which does, admittedly, imply death. Even so... it's still implied, not stated. As we'll see later, it's hard to count some of these characters out until we read a detailed description of their corpses.

The central point of all this is that various unknown factors taking place in this scene make it difficult to judge exactly what happened. That said, it's still not looking good for Jon. When all you can feel is cold, that's generally not an indication of premium health. So let's assume for the moment that Jon really has been stabbed to death. Does that mean he's down for the count? Hardly.

Jon's final word is "Ghost," a fact whose significance should not be underestimated. Among its other revelations, *A Dance with Dragons* gave readers more information about skinchangers and the powers of wargs, through the prologue perspective of Varamyr Sixskins. From Varamyr, we know that for his – and Jon's – kind, death is far from final.

> *Haggon's rough voice echoed in his head. "You will die a dozen deaths, boy, and every one will hurt... but when your true death comes, you will live again. The second life is simpler and sweeter, they say."*

> *Varamyr had died nine times before. He had died once from a spear thrust, once with a bear's teeth in his throat, and once in a wash of blood as he brought forth a stillborn cub. He died his first death when he was only six, as his father's axe crashed through his skull.*

*None of them had been as strong as Varamyr Sixskins, though, not even Haggon, tall and grim with his hands as hard as stone. The hunter died weeping after Varamyr took Greyskin from him, driving him out to claim the beast for his own.* No second life for you, old man.

*"They say you forget," Haggon had told him, a few weeks before his own death. "When the man's flesh dies, his spirit lives on inside the beast, but every day his memory fades, and the beast becomes a little less a warg, a little more a wolf, until nothing of the man is left and only the beast remains."*

*A Dance with Dragons*, Prologue

These quotes offer our first confirmation that skinchangers live on inside the animals they control after death. From what can be gleaned of the "rules" of this element of fantasy, it seems that skinchangers experience death to varying degrees. They can survive wearing the skin of an animal as the animal dies, though it pains them; Varamyr's claim to have died nine times before is testament to this. True death, however, apparently refers to the death of the skinchanger himself, after which time he enters "the second life." From what Varamyr tells us, and from what he himself experiences during the transition from his dying body to the body of one of his wolves, the second life involves the skinchanger's consciousness existing inside his beast until, thanks to the passage of time, his own persona is eventually consumed and he becomes the animal completely.

Even before Varamyr's prologue, we've seen a little of this phenomenon in the form of Orell, the wildling skinchanger that Jon killed and who took his hatred with him into his eagle. Varamyr's testimony, however, makes it (somewhat) official: when a skinchanger dies, his consciousness is transferred to the body of his beast. Since Jon's status as a warg is not in dispute, it stands to reason that when Jon was stabbed to death, his mind went into Ghost. According to Varamyr, it takes some time before the warg forgets who he is and becomes a wolf in truth; as a result, Jon's death need not be taken to mean the end of his story. Indeed, many are already speculating that *The Winds of Winter* will include chapters featuring the POV title of "Ghost." If this does occur, however, it's not expected to last, as there is any number of contrivances which could see Jon returned to his human form after spending some time in his direwolf's body. Either way, his role in *A Song of Ice and Fire* will continue.

There is at least one theory that could conceivably annul this course of events. The idea is that Wick, Bowen Marsh, and the rest of the people who stab Jon are not acting of their own volition, but instead are under the influence of Borroq, the wildling with the boar. Borroq, it seems, has been around for a long time; Varamyr recalls meeting him at a skinchanger gathering when he was ten-years-old. Considering Borroq's age and reputation (in the *Dance* appendix, he is described only as "much feared"), it's entirely possible that he can take control of multiple humans at once. We've already seen Bran take over Hodor's skin, and Bran hasn't been at this skinchanging game very long at all. This could explain Wick's contention, toward the end, that it wasn't him. Furthermore, if Borroq is the one trying to kill Jon, it's reasonable to think that he wants to take Jon's second life, as well. Borroq refers to Jon as "brother" upon their first meeting, suggesting that he knows Jon is a warg. Maybe the poison on Wick's knife is something that will deny Jon his second life, or maybe Borroq is attempting to accomplish that in some other fashion. In any case, the result would be true and final death for Jon.

This particular theory is included simply as an example of how far speculation can go. There's no real evidence to support Borroq's antagonism; he's never made himself out to be Jon's enemy, and we're only guessing at what he can do because of how experienced he seems to be. The theory exists, like so many others in *Song of Ice and Fire* fandom, because it can be made to fit the circumstances. And the reason for that is because the circumstances are so murky as to allow for a multitude of potential interpretations. Once again, there are simply too many possibilities, given everything at work in the situation.

The last of these situational factors is appropriately representative of ice and fire. The suspected magicks of the Wall are still mysterious, their true power unknown – if, indeed, there is any there at all. The Wall is frequently said to defend itself against attackers and has been demonstrably effective at keeping certain kinds of creatures from passing through. Most recently, dead men killed by the Others failed to rise as wights when kept in the ice cells of the Wall. This is a completely uncertain source of help for Jon, but it should not be totally discounted. If nothing else, perhaps it will keep his corpse fresh while he does time as a direwolf.

Meanwhile, a more direct solution exists in the form of Melisandre of Asshai. If there's one thing readers have learned by now, it's that anyone who dies in the vicinity of a cleric of R'hllor has instant access to a potential extra life. We know these people can reanimate the dead. We've witnessed the results. And that was when the likes of Thoros of Myr and Beric Dondarrion were performing it – Melisandre is supposedly one of the most powerful members of her order. From her own perspective:

> There was no one, even in her order, who had her skill at seeing the secrets half-revealed and half-concealed within the sacred flames.

> *A Dance with Dragons,* Melisandre I

And later in the same chapter, she contemplates how much stronger she is now that she is at the Wall, another indication of that structure's power:

> She was stronger at the Wall, stronger even than in Asshai. Her every word and gesture was more potent, and she could do things that she had never done before. Such shadows as I bring forth here will be terrible, and no creature of the dark will stand before them. *With such sorceries at her command, she should soon have no more need of the feeble tricks of alchemists and pyromancers.*

So, basically, it's a good bet that anything Thoros can do, Melisandre can do better. How could Jon possibly be allowed to stay dead? Melisandre has shown considerable interest in him already. Indeed, if she weren't so blindly devoted to Stannis Baratheon, she might soon see that interest increase exponentially. The full details of Melisandre's prophecy regarding Azor Ahai reborn, and why certain characters are better candidates for the role than Stannis, is not something that can feasibly be discussed here. Suffice it to say that the circumstances surrounding Jon's death can be seen, with some imagination, to fulfill various aspects of the supposed chosen one's return – the "bleeding star" refers to Ser Patrek of King's Mountain, the salt and smoke to Bowen Marsh's tears and Jon's wound that "seemed to smoke," etc. Given his connections with this prophecy, along with Melisandre herself and the strengthening power of the Wall, the idea that Jon died in the manner he did, in the place he did, in the situation he did, *and* that he'll actually stay dead is nearly inconceivable. There are just too many ways for him to come back.

### *The Narrative Argument: Plot Armor*

Up to now, we've kept this discussion strictly in storyland. We've talked about various magical rules systems, the resurrection powers of the red priests – all the myriad possibilities and creative loopholes that would keep Jon Snow in the game from an in-book perspective. But for every argument made supporting a possibility for Jon's revival, another can be made, perhaps equally as convincingly, for his permanent death. The Borroq theory is one of these. We are speculating wildly on what has occurred previously and will occur in the future, knowing full well that we don't have all the information and that any innovative plot twist in book six could render all our carefully-crafted analysis moot. We are guessing.

There is one argument, however, that provides more hard evidence than any other for Jon's continued existence. This argument is not about the story – it's about the structure of the story, and the pattern that structure has revealed over the years about who is in real danger and who isn't.

Here is the bottom line: Jon Snow isn't dead because he's still an important character. His arc isn't over. He has things to do, pasts to unravel, mysteries to solve, enemies to fight. He might be spoken of in prophecy as the reincarnation of an ancient warrior. He could very well be of trueborn royal blood, directly in line for the Iron Throne. His story isn't finished. In other words, he has plot armor.

In proper fashion, I hear you argue, "It's not that kind of series. Nobody has plot armor. People die all the time. Important characters die for no reason in these books. It's part of the author's whole gimmick; anyone could go at any second. Nobody saw Ned Stark's decapitation coming, or the Red Wedding. Jon is one of those characters who was almost destined to die early in these books, because he's an honorable person that the reader cheers for, and, as a result, he can't be suffered to live. Haven't we learned anything after all these years?"

To which you receive the polite, but firm, response: apologies, but you're wrong. As a matter of fact, while being a POV character in *A Song of Ice and Fire* can often be a harrowing business, the POVs do not die nearly as often as they are *teased* as dying. Here's the proof.

## False Character Death

False character death refers, here, to the literary practice of ending a chapter on a life-or-death cliffhanger and/or implying that a major character has died and making the reader wait to find out if it's true. In *Ice and Fire*, it happens *a lot*. To demonstrate the frequency of this sort of occurrence, we must break down the series, book by book, in order to find it.

In *A Game of Thrones*, we started out with eight POV characters. Six of these are members of the Stark family: Eddard, Catelyn, Sansa, Arya, Bran, and Jon Snow. The other two are Tyrion Lannister and Daenerys Targaryen. Over the course of the book, three of these characters have brushes with death from a reader's perspective:

> *Screaming, Bran went backward out the window into empty air. There was nothing to grab on to. The courtyard rushed up to meet him.*

> *A Game of Thrones*, Bran II

This is our first taste of Mr. Martin's bloodthirsty sense of realism. Bran's is the first actual POV chapter of the series. In his second chapter, he is flung from a window, and the immediate context makes it seem as though he might have died. Even after we discover that he's barely survived, he has to wake up from his coma, and then he's crippled from the waist down. There's a reason this was chosen as the final scene of HBO's pilot episode – it's our first indication of the nature of the series. Not even children are safe here.

*As the blade flashed toward her face, Arya threw herself backward, kicking wildly, wrenching her head from side to side, but he had her by the hair, so strong, she could feel her scalp tearing, and on her lips the salt taste of tears.*

*A Game of Thrones*, Arya V

This is, technically speaking, the chapter in which Eddard Stark dies, though we don't get confirmation of that until the next chapter, in which Bran and Rickon dream about it, and then the one after that, in which Sansa sees the head. This is also Arya's final appearance in the book; coming directly on the heels of Ned's death, it certainly gives the impression that Yoren is about to cut her throat. This is the first instance in the series of a POV character ending a book on a desperate note, only to turn up alive later on. In Arya's case, hers is the first POV chapter of *A Clash of Kings*.

Keep in mind that the proof of Martin's remorselessness regarding his characters does not just come at the expense of POV characters – far from it. Over the course of *Game*, we witness the deaths of major characters Viserys Targaryen, Robert Baratheon, and Khal Drogo. Take this with the crippling of Bran, the execution of Ned Stark (the novel's chief protagonist), and Arya's cliffhanger ending, and it becomes clear why readers got the sense that in this brutal and realistic fantasy setting, no character is safe.

*Clash* adds two new POVs: Theon Greyjoy and Davos Seaworth. It also contains three more teasing "death" scenes.

*"Gods be good," he said softly. "Both of them?"*

*"I fear so, my lord.    It is so sad.    So grievous sad.    And them so young and innocent."*

*A Clash of Kings*, Tyrion XII

This is the first word readers get that Bran and Rickon have been killed at Theon's hand.  The emotional impact of this incident comes to a height in the next chapter, in which we get a first-hand look at Catelyn's reaction.  In the chapter after that, however, Theon's perspective makes it clear that he did not, in fact, murder the Stark boys.  For readers, Bran's false death is brief but notable, often eliciting a fairly extreme reaction.  It's all the more notable because Bran's continued survival has now been called into serious question twice in as many books.

*Davos could make out the striped hulls of Salladhor Saan's ships beyond, but he knew he would never reach them.  A wall of red-hot steel, blazing wood, and swirling green flame stretched before him. The mouth of the Blackwater Rush had turned into the mouth of hell.*

*A Clash of Kings*, Davos III

Granted, there's nothing here to explicitly suggest that Davos is dead.  However, he does end *Clash* in a seemingly inescapable situation, and his final chapter can be considered a cliffhanger. When he reappears in *A Storm of Swords*, his survival is generally considered somewhat miraculous.

> *The last thing Theon Greyjoy saw was Smiler, kicking free of the burning stables with his mane ablaze, screaming, rearing...*

> A Clash of Kings, Theon VI

There doesn't seem to be a lot of ambiguity here. It's the final sentence of Theon's final chapter in *Clash*, and it includes the phrase "the last thing Theon Greyjoy saw," which tends to be a giveaway. It's a long way into *Storm* before we can confirm that Theon is alive at all, and he doesn't appear again in any sense until *Dance*. This presents one of the more extreme (though not the *most* extreme) examples of false character death: Theon ends *Clash of Kings* in a manner that clearly suggests his demise, and, for a while, there's no reason to believe any differently.

By the end of *Clash*, two characters have experienced a false death followed by a confirmation of survival. We learn in the beginning that Arya survived her encounter with Yoren from the first book, and we learn at the end the details of Bran's escape. Even so, however, the series has not reneged on its promises of realism via characters' deaths. Theon looks like a goner, and the book has already claimed the life of Renly Baratheon, not to mention lesser characters such as Qhorin Halfhand. If that weren't enough, Catelyn Stark ends the novel with her sword at the throat of Jaime Lannister; he might not be a POV character quite yet, but he certainly ends the book on a life-or-death moment. There still isn't much of a reason to doubt the likelihood of the deaths of major characters.

Two more new POVs join the party in *A Storm of Swords*:    Jaime and Samwell Tarly. Jaime actually follows the trend established by Arya in the second book; from an apparently desperate situation, his appearance as a POV character in the first chapter of the novel provides the evidence that he has survived.  And as long as we're following trends, *Storm* once again provides three instances of false character death:

> *Only when he grasped the offered hand did he realize that the rider wore no glove. His hand was black and cold, with fingers hard as stone.*

> *A Storm of Swords*, Samwell III

Whether or not anyone actually believed this was Sam's death scene is debatable, but it is a life-or-death cliffhanger ending to the chapter. We know nothing about Coldhands at this point – the black hands of Sam's "rescuer" seem to bode tremendously ill.  It's ten more chapters before Bran's perspective clues us in that Sam and Gilly made it out alive, and that Coldhands is more than what he seemed.

> *Then the steel was at her throat, and its bite was red and cold.*

> *A Storm of Swords*, Catelyn VII

This is the big one, probably the furthest Martin has yet gone in the series to fake the death of a major character – because, of course, the death of Catelyn Stark isn't faked at all.  She dies (the only POV character thus far who actually dies in one of his or her own chapters), and then she comes back to life.  Some will be tempted to make the argument that Cat can't be said to have survived, since the person she was is pretty much dead and buried, and Lady Stoneheart is someone else entirely.  This is, however, something of a technicality and doesn't apply here.  Catelyn Stark is still walking and (sort of) talking, she still has a role to play, and she's still part of the story.  Here, we see one of the best examples of the notion that you can't trust anything you read when it comes to the deaths of POVs.

*His axe took her in the back of the head.*

*A Storm of Swords*, Arya XI

Okay, so it was the flat.  Still, at the risk of repetition:    life-or-death cliffhanger chapter ending.  And, really, think about the placement of this chapter in the book.  This comes directly after the Red Wedding; Arya XI begins immediately following Catelyn's death.   For readers, how difficult could it possibly have been to imagine that, given his sadistic tendencies, Martin swept Arya along to her final reward along with the other Starks in the immediate vicinity?  If there was ever a time to buy into the idea that Arya had just been killed by a man like Sandor Clegane, it was right after her mother and brother had been slaughtered.

And, of course, *Storm* is chock-full of non-POV deaths.  In addition to Robb Stark, whose loss cut deepest, Balon Greyjoy, Joffrey Baratheon, Tywin Lannister, Shae, Ygritte, Jeor Mormont, Dontos Hollard, Oberyn Martell, and Lysa Arryn all bit the dust in this one.  Eight out of those 11 names had been important characters since book one.

So what were the conclusions coming out of the original three novels, in regards to the likelihood of major characters snuffing it? Clearly, characters were going to die, and they were probably going to die often – having a crown on your head only seemed to hasten the end. That said, does it help to be a POV character in this series? The first instinct of most readers is to say no, but the fact of the matter is that, yes, it does. Think about it: at this point, we've had a total of 12 POVs. Seven of them – more than half – have experienced false deaths via cliffhanger endings, after which, it turns out, they survived (or, in Catelyn's case, they just kind of ignored the whole dying thing). Arya and Bran each experienced this sort of thing twice.

So, all told, there have been nine instances of false character deaths for POVs versus one instance of true death. Yes, Westeros tends to be a pretty deadly place, but it is starting to seem a lot easier to scrape your way out of the grave if any chapters begin with your name.

Everything got more complicated upon the release of *A Feast for Crows*. Not only did we get new POVs in the form of Cersei and Brienne, but we also started to get a different, perhaps lesser, form of POV chapter. These are the characters who generally have two to four chapters per book, initially fascinating because of the looks they gave readers at Dorne and the Iron Islands, and particularly distinguished by their titles, which are not the names of the characters themselves but, rather, some sort of descriptive phrase which changes with each chapter. Arianne Martell, for instance, saw her chapters in *Feast* respectively named "The Queenmaker" and "The Princess in the Tower." Moreover, *A Dance with Dragons* continued this trend of non-eponymous-POVs, so that by the time the two most recent books were over, the total count of character POVs had jumped into the 20s – but nine of these didn't get to use their own names as chapter titles.

And, as it turns out, that's just not as safe.

*The white knight raised his blade, too slowly. Hotah's longaxe took his right arm off at the shoulder, spun away spraying blood, and came flashing back again in a terrible two-handed slash that removed the head of Arys Oakheart and sent it spinning through the air.*

*A Feast for Crows*, The Queenmaker

Prior to this scene, Arys Oakheart had received one POV chapter of his own, called "The Soiled Knight." Seven total chapters went by between the introduction of his perspective and his severed head sinking into the Greenblood, but he was technically a POV character, however briefly, and, technically, he died and has not come back. Like Ned Stark, the only other previous POV character to accomplish this feat, Ser Arys did not die in his own chapter.

*"Your Grace, glad tidings,"' he announced. "Wyman Manderly has done as you commanded and beheaded Lord Stannis's onion knight."*

*"We know this for a certainty?"*

*"The man's head and hands have been mounted about the walls of White Harbor. Lord Wyman avows this, and the Freys confirm. They have seen the head there, with an onion in its mouth. And the*

*hands, one marked by his shortened fingers."*

*A Feast for Crows*, Cersei V

Davos Seaworth is back in the false death business in *Feast*, as demonstrated by this dialogue which indicates that he has been beheaded off-screen. Due to the gap between the fourth and fifth books in the series, the fate of Davos was one of the more interesting topics during the long wait for *Dance*; it had been confirmed that he would have POV chapters, but the books overlap in time, and Davos's installments could have easily been a lead-up to his death, just as Cersei Lannister was told. As it turned out, this masterful trick in false death was actually a lead-up to... another case of false death.

*Brienne felt the hemp constricting, digging into her skin, jerking her chin upward. Ser Hyle was cursing them eloquently, but not the boy. Podrick never lifted his eyes, not even when his feet were jerked up off the ground.* If this is another dream, it is time for me to awaken. If this is real, it is time for me to die. *All she could see was Podrick, the noose around his thin neck, his legs twitching. Her mouth opened. Pod was kicking, choking, dying. Brienne sucked the air in desperately, even as the rope was strangling her. Nothing had ever hurt so much.*

*She screamed a word.*

*A Feast for Crows*, Brienne VIII

Like Davos, this was another commonly discussed "death" scene during the wait. Some believed Brienne's word had won her reprieve; others thought it had simply been her last word. The question was resolved in *Dance*, when she appeared briefly in that book's lone Jaime chapter. Again, the character with the chapter name makes it out alive.

> *When he opened his mouth to curse them all, black water filled his lungs, and the dark closed in around him.*

> *A Dance with Dragons*, Tyrion V

This is actually Tyrion Lannister's first and only false character death. Whether or not readers really believed this was it for the Imp, it was an ending to a chapter that suggested the distinct likelihood of death in a way that other Tyrion chapters hadn't. But as we already know, he turned out just fine. Jon Connington even caught the grayscale so Tyrion didn't have to.

> *"Cousin, take this creature to the Wolf's Den and cut off his head and hands. I want them brought to me before I sup. I shall not be able to eat a bite until I see this smuggler's head upon a spike, with an onion shoved between his lying teeth."*

> *A Dance with Dragons*, Davos III

Here we have Davos's false death derived from his previous false death, during his encounter with Wyman Manderly. Despite the implications of this passage matching up perfectly with the passage from *Feast*'s Cersei V, Manderly turns out to be a brilliant actor, and Davos makes it out of the Wolf's Den unscathed.

> If they take us alive, they will deliver us to Ramsay. *Theon grabbed Jeyne about her waist and jumped.*
>
> *A Dance with Dragons*, Theon I

This isn't necessarily a fake death scene, but it certainly has that same sort of feeling to it with the "if they take us alive" thought preceding the jump. Furthermore, these are the last lines of the chapter, and we don't know that Theon and Jeyne survived until the end of "The Sacrifice," well over a hundred pages later.

> *The Dornish prince was three days dying. He took his last shuddering breath in the bleak black dawn, as cold rain hissed from a dark sky to turn the bricks of the old city into rivers.*
>
> *A Dance with Dragons*, The Queen's Hand

The third and final POV character to die an apparent actual death is Quentyn Martell. Quentyn had four chapters in *Dance* under non-eponymous titles. He died in the same book in which his POV was introduced (just like Ned and Arys), and he died in someone else's chapter (in this case, one of Barristan Selmy's). Like Arys Oakheart, his death had comparatively little impact, particularly when measured against the potential demise of someone like Jon Snow.

And, finally, while there was never a plausible chance that she was actually gone for good, Daenerys Targaryen spends a significant amount of time in *Dance with Dragons* off-screen and presumed dead.

So.

Leaving aside prologue and epilogue characters whose deaths are assured, there are 24 POVs. Of these:

- Four have been legitimately killed: Eddard Stark, Catelyn Stark, Arys Oakheart, and Quentyn Martell.
- One of those, Catelyn, has returned from the grave.
- Eight have been put into narrative circumstances in which readers could reasonably infer that they have been killed but later turned out to have survived: Arya Stark (twice), Bran Stark (twice), Theon Greyjoy (twice), Sam Tarly, Davos Seaworth (thrice), Brienne of Tarth, Tyrion Lannister, and Daenerys Targaryen.
- This makes three dead POV characters, as opposed to nine not-so-dead ones.

It's been made abundantly clear: while Martin's universe is often a heartless and deadly one, having chapters with your name on them effectively straps your survival odds to a rocket ship. What we've found is incontrovertible evidence that, popular belief aside, the death of a POV character is an extremely rare occurrence.

So what do these trends say about the chances that Jon Snow is actually dead?

1. The total number of actual POV character deaths (three) pales in comparison to the total number of false POV deaths (15 total incidents). The

number of not-so-dead characters (nine) is triple the number of characters who have stayed dead.

2.  More than a third of all POV characters have experienced false character death. An eighth of POV characters have experienced true death.

3.  Of the three POVs who have stayed dead, all were introduced as POVs in the same book they died in. Of the original eight POVs (in which Jon is included), Ned Stark is the only one who has died for good.

4.  Ned Stark is also the only dead POV character with eponymous chapters.

5.  Every POV character who has died has done so from someone else's perspective, with the exception of Catelyn Stark, who later returned. Jon's supposed death occurred in his own chapter.

6.  The total combined number of chapters for the POV characters who have stayed dead is 21. Jon has amassed 42 chapters (double that amount) himself over the course of the series.

Conclusion? It's no contest. Jon Snow is a long-time POV character, and he's not going anywhere – yet. The myriad of different ways in which he could get out of his seemingly fatal situation is one thing, but when you analyze the narrative structure and consider everything that Jon still has to do as a character in this story, you realize that his death at the end of *A Dance with Dragons* isn't just unlikely – it's practically impossible. Whether he comes back as a wolf or gets zombified by Melisandre or just survives the attack for some previously unforeseen reason, he will continue to have a major role in *A Song of Ice and Fire*. The final scene of *Dance*'s Jon XIII is a false death, not the real thing.

Of course, as we get closer to the end of the series, these statistics will begin to lose meaning as the stakes of the story get higher and characters start to complete their arcs. Jon Snow is no exception to that, and he may well be destined for ultimate death in the final installment. Until then, however, don't believe anything you read – about his death, or Arya's, or Tyrion's, or Dany's, or any of those people whose eyes we've been looking through since *A Game of Thrones*. As much as some might like to deny it, this is still a fantasy story, and these people are still Our Heroes. That's why they're still around despite their near-constant brushes with doom, and that's why they'll still be around for the endgame. There's no story without them.

# THE PRINCE THAT ILLYRIO PROMISED

*Exploring the identity of – and the aim of the conspiracy around – Aegon Targaryen*

Alexander Smith

> *"Aegon," he said to a woman nursing a newborn babe in a great wooden bed. "What better name for a king?"*
>
> *"Will you make a song for him?" the woman asked.*
>
> *"He has a song," the man replied. "He is the prince that was promised, and his is the song of ice and fire."*

*A Clash of Kings*, Daenerys IV

The death of Aegon Targaryen, the son of Prince Rhaegar, shook the Seven Kingdoms for years to come. It nearly drove a permanent wedge between Eddard Stark and Robert Baratheon, which was only healed by the death of Lyanna. It helped drive Ned's distrust of Tywin Lannister, setting the stage for a feud that would, some 15 years later, tear the realm apart. And it so haunted Lord Eddard that he felt compelled to warn Cersei that he knew the truth about the incestuous parentage of her children, which proved to be the catalyst that toppled his house and accelerated the War of the Five Kings.

And yet, after all these reverberations across the lands of Westeros and Essos across all these years, we learned in *A Dance with Dragons* that Aegon was actually alive, biding his time in secret until the right opportunity to claim his birthright presented itself. By the end of that book, Aegon's invasion has finally commenced – which will almost certainly play a substantial role in the final stretch of the story – but is this pale-haired youth really what he seems?

The answer is almost certainly not.

If one takes Aegon at face value, the story is apparently thus: Illyrio Mopatis, a Magister of Pentos who used to be a bravo, and Varys, a spymaster who used to be a thief, decided for reasons not fully revealed that the Targaryen dynasty should not end in Westeros. Therefore, when the fall of King's Landing appeared imminent, Varys switched out Aegon for another baby and spirited him to safety with Illyrio in Pentos. The magister then protected him, procured tutors for him in every field from martial pursuits to the Faith, and made arrangements with the Golden Company to bring him to power in Westeros when the time was right.

But then there are complications. Years later, Illyrio also took in the last known Targaryens, Viserys and Daenerys, and arranged a marriage to bring a Dothraki *khalasar* into the mix, as well. Apparently, he planned to have this merry band of barbarians and mercenaries invade Westeros and live happily ever after. Illyrio himself would become master of coin and take any castle of his choosing in the Seven Kingdoms as his seat.

It's a neat little story, as far as stories go, but as an actual, decades-long strategy, it's full of holes. First of all, why would a magister of Pentos care about events across the sea? He already has enough wealth and power in his native city to satisfy any man. Both Tywin and Tyrion Lannister, generally shrewd judges of character, believe the rich in the Free Cities care naught for land or titles or vassals and are merely hoarders of wealth. Daenerys's impressions of Illyrio during her half-year stay indicate that he is a merchant interested in acquiring wealth through trade in luxury goods and would sell out anyone for the right price. Even Illyrio himself, when asked by Tyrion why he would care about Westeros, can only suggest that he appreciates the gold he would handle as master of coin, but is greed a sufficient motivator for a plan that is already some 18 years in progress? Tyrion, for one, believes this motivation to be suspect.

Then there is his treatment of Viserys and Daenerys. Here is a man conspiring to put a Targaryen back on the throne in the form of Aegon, but he has no real backup plan if Aegon fails. Still, while Illyrio hid him for over a decade, he let Viserys and Daenerys wander from Free City to Free City and squander what few possessions they had. He let Viserys gain the moniker "the Beggar King" and lose the respect of all the power brokers on Essos. He left the pair vulnerable to assassins that could have realistically been pursuing them if Jon Arryn had not convinced King Robert to stay his hand. Even when he finally did decide to shelter the pair, he did not seem to care if they lived or died. Hell, by his own admission, he gave Daenerys up for dead the moment he brokered the marriage with Khal Drogo. Sure, Aegon was the focus, but if Illyrio was really concerned about House Targaryen as a ruling entity, why did he pay so little attention to the rest of the family?

And the plan itself is, upon reflection, a bit of a stretch, to put it mildly (something which has bothered me since the moment I first read *Game of Thrones*). Viserys Targaryen, the exiled son of a madman deposed from the throne in part for his penchant for burning people alive, is going to form a barbarian horde, conquer the Seven Kingdoms in a manner that will probably involve a whole lot of Dothraki raping, looting, and pillaging, and then rule to the end of his days after those same Dothraki return to their grasslands. Really? Sure, Aegon I was a foreign conqueror that took Westeros through fire and blood, but he controlled the means to secure his rule: dragons. While Illyrio gave Daenerys three dragon eggs, there is no indication that he actually expected them to hatch – and, even if he did, he wanted Viserys to remain in Pentos and never expected Daenerys to return, leaving no one behind to tend to them.

Even Jorah Mormont, a Northerner with more brawn and tenacity than brains, cannot see how the Dothraki, who despise siegecraft and believe the best strategy against massed infantry is a full-frontal charge – even if said infantry consists of ranks of cavalry-obliterating pikemen or could easily be flanked – could conquer Westeros. If Illyrio and Varys really thought that Viserys – or anyone, for that matter – could conquer and hold a land the size of South America with a rented *khalasar*, then they are not nearly as cunning as Martin has led us to believe.

So if Illyrio's motives and methods both appear to make little sense, what is actually going on? Well, here is the situation as I see it. When Illyrio Mopatis was a young man, he teamed up with Varys to become such an important information broker in the city that he was able to wed a relative of the prince of Pentos and become a magister. He now had money, power, and respect, but then he married his second wife, Serra. According to his conversation with Tyrion, this marriage was for love, and this statement appears genuine; after all, he did save her hands in his bedchamber, an extreme measure for just a passing fling. Furthermore, he sacrificed much in power and influence to conclude the match, as the gates of the prince's palace were, in his words, forever closed to him. Finally, as a worker in a Lysene pleasure house, it appears that Serra was most likely a slave, which would certainly make her an unsuitable wife in the status-conscious Free Cities. There can be no question that he really did love his wife greatly, and there can equally be no question that the union wasn't popular in the city.

So, what would happen if Illyrio and Serra had a son? This question is impossible to answer definitively since we do not have all the facts we require regarding Pentoshi culture, but some plausible outcomes can be postulated. Firstly, he would automatically earn the enmity of the 40 families from which the prince of Pentos is chosen, for if Illyrio earned their scorn by setting aside his connections with the prince of Pentos to marry a slave, then one can only imagine what these families would think of a spawn of that union running about. I do not think that would be pleasant for the child at all, at any point in his life.

Secondly, he would probably be ridiculed by wider Pentoshi society. While the city does appear to encourage upward mobility, judging by Illyrio's acceptance as a leading citizen, there is no evidence that slaves are encouraged to be upwardly mobile. While the Pentoshi stance towards slaves is clearly not as harsh as Volantis's, where tattoos help ensure that pure-blooded Volantenes and slaves will never mix, both cities come from the same Valyrian stock, and there appears to be a firm dividing line between slaves and nobles throughout that culture. I, therefore, find it unlikely that a boy with some slave blood in him would be welcomed in Pentoshi society even without the complication of Illyrio's relationship with the 40 families. Put the two circumstances together, and his options appear truly limited. While this hypothetical child would presumably still inherit Illyrio's massive fortune, he would, in all likelihood, face major obstacles in thriving in his native city – or, indeed, in any of the Free Cities, which are all slave states (save for Braavos), as well. Under these circumstances, Illyrio would have to look elsewhere to provide opportunities for his son.

And if he's going to create a new persona with a new set of possibilities open for him, why not go all the way and reach for the highest pinnacle currently available to the modern, post-Valyrian world? Based on the above musings, I strongly believe that Illyrio decided to take advantage of events to crown his son king of Westeros as a Targaryen pretender. In this scenario, the plan would have been launched soon after the sack of King's Landing. From his friend Varys, serving in the capital, Illyrio has learned that baby Aegon was not only killed, but had his head bashed in and his face ruined. As luck would have it, Illyrio had recently fathered a son. This would make an infant-switching story plausible.

Of course, Illyrio's son needed to have the Targaryen look for this scheme to work, but this is also well within the realm of possibility. There's always the stalwart Varys, the former mummer, to lend a hand in this department, but he may not have had to; we know Serra sported golden hair streaked with silver, and the color could have easily been inherited from her. And "Aegon" could have received her blue eyes, too – I am not convinced that he actually has purple eyes. When Tyrion first meets him, Aegon's eyes appear dark blue most of the time, but they can also appear black or purple under the right light. This is put down to his dyed hair making his eyes look different, but even after he returns to his natural silver locks, his eyes are still described as being not as purple as Rhaegar's. If his eyes are really that difficult to place on the spectrum, it's entirely possible they are not actually purple at all, and his Targaryen look is a fabrication.

Wanting to place his son on the throne makes much more sense than Illyrio wanting to gather more riches in Westeros. As the rightful king of Westeros, the lad would have the kind of promising future that a loving father would want for his son, and there are certainly hints that Illyrio's affection for the boy runs deep. Tyrion hears genuine disappointment in Illyrio's voice when the magister learns he will be unable to see "Young Griff" before the boy begins his journey down the Rhoyne to Volantis. His shoulders are also slumped as he watches Tryrion, Haldon, and Duck leave for Ghoyan Drohe. Finally, Illyrio even brought a bag of the boy's favorite sweets along as a gift. This amount of care and disappointment appears out of place coming from a man Daenerys has heard would sell any of his friends for the right price.

Illyrio's treatment of Viserys and Daenerys also makes far more sense in this light. If Illyrio cares nothing for a Targaryen restoration and merely wants his own son on the throne, he would definitely not be troubled if Viserys died or Daenerys was sold into child slavery. Furthermore, they become useful distractions for King Robert to focus on while he swings a deal with the Golden Company and works with the supposedly dead Jon Connington to raise Aegon as a prince.

Even the Dothraki invasion makes more sense in this context. Perhaps Viserys was being set up as the fall guy. A half-mad Targaryen with a Dothraki horde strikes fear in the hearts of the Westerosi. As Jorah notes to Daenerys, the Dothraki have no ability with siegecraft and will probably be unable to conquer the Seven Kingdoms, but they will reap great destruction. Then, when people begin losing hope, Aegon is revealed at the head of the Golden Company and rallies the forces of Westeros to drive the Dothraki out and kill Mad Viserys. This allows Aegon to return as a hero rather than as a conqueror.

While much of the above is merely speculation, Martin has provided key clues of his own that indicate Aegon may not be the Targaryen he appears to be. The first of these clues comes in *A Clash of Kings*, well before Aegon has even been introduced. Among the many visions Daenerys sees in the House of the Undying while the warlock leaders attempt to feed on her is a cloth dragon swaying on poles before a cheering crowd. This implies a fake dragon being presented to the people of Westeros. The Undying also call her "slayer of lies" after showing her this vision, as well as a vision of Stannis, implying that she has some false kings and false chosen ones she needs to expose. The second clue comes in *A Dance with Dragons* itself as Quaithe describes dangerous people Daenerys will meet in the near future. One of these is identified as "the mummer's dragon," which has an uncanny resemblance to the vision in the House of the Undying. And, finally, a tie to Varys is strongly implied, since Varys himself is a mummer and is in league with Aegon. While neither of these prophesies is conclusive, they do cast reasonable suspicion that Aegon is not who he seems.

Still don't buy into the whole concept? Let's go a little farther afield and examine some of Martin's more general MOs. He does appear to like the switched identity bit. For instance, Jeyne Pool became Arya Stark at the behest of Lord Tywin so the Lannisters could corral the North and the Boltons could consolidate their claim on the wardenship, certainly a similar ploy to the one I have accused Illyrio of instigating. Also, one of our central characters, a certain Mr. Jon Snow, is more than likely not the bastard son of Eddard Stark and may carry a secret heritage of his own.

Martin also likes to play with prophecy and character interpretation of prophecy. Daenerys' son, Rhaego, was supposed to be the "Stallion Who Mounts the World," yet he died in the womb. Stannis Baratheon was supposed to win a great victory at King's Landing because Renly was no longer alive to lead a host to crush him beneath the walls of the city, as Melisandre saw in her flames, yet Renly was there in spirit through Ser Garlan Tyrell, who wore the dead pretender's armor to inspire the troops at the Blackwater. Melisandre thought the prophecy of Azor Ahai reborn must refer to Dragonstone, yet there are now two separate events, the birth of Daenerys' dragons and the assassination of Jon Snow, that appear to fulfill the requirements of Azor Ahai being born again under a bleeding star amidst smoke and salt. It would be fitting, then, if Rhaegar, too, was mistaken when he believed that Aegon was the Prince That Was Promised.

Finally, we know Martin likes to draw from English history, particularly the Wars of the Roses, when shaping many of the characters and events in Westeros, so I think it is relevant to point out a potential historical parallel, a pretender to the English throne named Perkin Warbeck.

First, a bit of background is necessary. In April 1483, Edward IV of England died, and his brother, Richard, Duke of Gloucester, became lord protector for Edward's twelve-year-old son, Edward V. Two months later, however, evidence emerged that Edward IV, a notorious womanizer and one of the inspirations for the character of Robert Baratheon, may have promised a woman named Eleanor Talbot that he would marry her in order to convince the noblewoman to sleep with him. Under Church law, this pre-contract would render his actual marriage to Elizabeth Woodville null and void and make Edward V and his younger brother, Richard, illegitimate. When news of this earlier dalliance became public, Edward was stripped of his titles and Richard III became the lord protector. Edward and Prince Richard were then confined to the Tower of London, from which they never emerged alive. While their fates have never been conclusively proven, many believed that Richard III had them murdered to protect his claim to the throne.

This would have been the end of the tale of the princes in the tower if not for the aforementioned Warbeck, the son of a Flemish official from Torunai. Possessing a similar appearance to Prince Richard, Perkin declared himself the rightful king of England in 1490 and landed in Kent with a small army in 1495 to press his claim. This invasion ultimately failed. After a second failed uprising in 1497, he was captured, revealed as a pretender, and executed.

The similarities here are striking. Assuming for the moment that our young Targaryen really is Illyrio's son, we have Aegon, the heir to the throne, killed much like Richard, the younger of the two children, to solidify the

Baratheon claim to the Iron Throne.  Then, after some years have passed, we have the son of an official in the Free Cities – which, in terms of their proximity and trade relationships with the English analogue of Westeros, most closely resemble the prosperous trading cities of the Low Countries, such as Warbeck's own Tournai – who happens to resemble the dead prince declaring himself the king.  While we cannot be certain that Martin is drawing from this particular episode in crafting the story of Aegon, doing so would jive with his penchant for reenacting key moments in English history in *A Song of Ice and Fire*.

But, yes, there is still the possibility that I'm wrong, that I've fallen head-over-heels for a crackpot theory (though, to be fair, Aegon Targaryen surviving Robert's Rebellion was a crackpot theory not all that long ago).  Certainly, none of the evidence is conclusive.  Aegon does appear to have the Targaryen look.   Varys possesses the requisite skills and resources to have easily switched babies during the sack of King's Landing.  Illyrio is fond of the boy, yes, but Aegon need not be his natural son for the magister to have grown attached to him while raising him in secret during his early childhood.

Furthermore, there are certainly hints that Aegon is important.   Even if Rhaegar erred in naming his son the Prince That Was Promised after he was born, we still have to contend with his belief that three Targaryen children were needed to stem the coming darkness.  This is why he cast aside his own bride, Elia Martell, so sickly she could no longer bear him any more children, for that fiery she-wolf, Lyanna Stark.  Assuming Jon Snow is a Targaryen, then Daenerys needs one more real McCoy if Rhaegar is to be believed.  Maester Aemon apparently thought the same thing, as he became desperate to cling to life as his body failed him in Braavos, since he thought Daenerys needed him and that the "dragon must have three heads."

There is also Kevan Lannister's final conversation with Varys to consider, in which Varys tells Kevan that Aegon is returning. The mortally wounded knight and the crossbow-wielding eunuch were alone during the last conversation of Kevan's life – not counting a little bird or six – so Varys would appear to have no motive to lie. One could even argue that Varys's taunting would be even more hurtful if he revealed that Aegon was a fake and that House Lannister would lose all its power to a mere pretender. Either way, it is certainly tempting to take Varys at his word in this instance.

Like Jon Snow's parentage, Illyrio and Varys's motivations in meddling in Westerosi affairs appears to be one of the central mysteries key to unraveling the core plot points of *A Song of Ice and Fire*. While Aegon really being Illyrio's son would not completely unravel this mystery – and there are still holes in the story that need to be filled in, even if it were true – this theory goes a long way towards explaining how Illyrio accidentally played a key role in Daenerys's transformation into the mother of dragons and the savior of Westeros from another Long Night.

# A GAME OF BEDS

*Marital infidelity, adultery, and fandom theories in* A Song of Ice and Fire

Amin Javadi

Marital infidelity is rampant in George R.R. Martin's *A Song of Ice and Fire* series. From Cersei Lannister's incestuous relationship and cuckolding of King Robert Baratheon to Rhaegar Targaryen's possible infidelity with Lyanna Stark, extramarital relationships have had significant political ramifications in Westerosi history. Infidelity and its consequences, in fact, are one of the major driving plot elements of the series. Examining the instances of such behavior, both known and speculative, provides insight into the functioning of the nobility in Westeros and the motivations of many characters in Martin's saga.

Adultery undercuts an important aspect of a nobleman's life in Westeros: siring legitimate heirs and ensuring the proper passing on of lands, titles, and powers. From Jon Snow to Ramsay Bolton, bastard children can throw a wrench into the regular procession of inheritance. It is by no mistake that bastards, often the children of adulterous relationships, are generally disdained throughout most of Westeros.[1] And even if there are no confirmed bastard children, the

---

[1] Dorne being a notable exception.

questioning of parentage created by infidelity – and even the speculation of infidelity – is very problematic and has played an important role in the narrative.

The preeminent example of marital infidelity in the novels is Queen Cersei Lannister's incestuous relationship with her brother, Ser Jaime Lannister. This extramarital relationship and the resulting bastard children are a major plot point in *A Game of Thrones* and have lasting consequences throughout the series. Cersei thought the wrong person came back from the Battle of the Trident but still went into her marriage willing to give it a chance. That initial resolve waivered during her wedding night, when the mental infidelity of Robert whispering Lyanna's name seriously undercut the beginning of their marriage. It crumbled with Robert's later physical infidelities, which shattered any chance of Cersei remaining faithful (though whether she would have permanently cut off her decades-long relationship with her twin can honestly be brought into question). Cersei recalls Robert's "playing around" with his Estermont cousin, which was the night where she welcomed Jaime into her bed to cuckold Robert and the night when Joffrey might have been conceived.

Parallel to Cersei's serial adultery runs Robert's lustful conquests. The king started siring bastards before his marriage and continued with abundance during his reign. The contrast in the status and danger of Robert and Cersei's behavior highlights the importance that one's sex makes in playing the game of beds. While Robert's bastard children could potentially make a difference in inheritance down the line, it is his prerogative and right to stray outside his marriage bed, like the male nobles sworn to him; society might frown on such behavior, but there are no legal punishments for it.    In contrast, Cersei and any other noblewoman outside of Dorne can pay for infidelity with their lives.  This blatant double standard is, of course, unfair and an example of the patriarchal system dominating the majority of Westeros and the majority of its institutions, including marriage.

Cersei attempts to take advantage of this male dominance by casting suspicion on Margaery Tyrell, her daughter-in-law and, in her eyes, a "younger and more beautiful queen" that she desperately wishes to be rid off.  The queen regent generates a significant amount of false evidence and is successful in having the Faith detain Margaery for trial.  The fandom jury is still out on whether Margaery is entirely innocent of these accusations; she may have lost her hymen, but as Cersei notes herself, this can happen through physical activity, like horseback riding.  Perhaps Renly did manage to claim her maidenhead, though we have no way of knowing for sure.  *If* Grand Maester Pycelle's testimony can be trusted, then Margaery made a request for moon tea, which confuses matters, particularly because we are unsure how exactly it works.  Is moon tea a contraceptive or an abortifacient?[2] Does it have any other effects on the female reproductive system, specifically menstruation? On A Podcast of Ice and Fire, we have discussed far-fetched ideas on this topic, including the unlikely-but-possible event of Margaery having aborted Renly's child.[3]

---

[2] If it was used to end Lysa Tully's pregnancy, it seems to have abortifacient properties.

[3] Amusingly, these discussions occurred on our Guys' Night Out episodes, where we were the least qualified to tackle them.  A "Tyrell moonblood" scenario was hypothesized in episode 69 by Elio Garcia, co-founder of Westeros.org, if

In any case, Cersei's attempt to play the system backfires on her, like most of her political scheming in *A Feast for Crows*. Her capture and upcoming trial by the Faith highlights the particular danger a noblewoman faces for having an extramarital affair, compared to simple "wanton fornication."[4] In *A Dance with Dragons*, Cersei confesses to taking Osney Kettleblack and Lancel as lovers after Robert's death. In fact, she over-confesses to include all three Kettleblack brothers amongst her list of lovers, doing so because she knows these actions did not constitute a capital crime. The High Septon summarizes the difference:

> *The wickedness of widows is well-known, and all women are wantons at heart, given to using their wiles and their beauty to work their wills on men. There is no treason here, so long as you did not stray from your marriage bed whilst His Grace King Robert was still alive.*
>
> *A Dance with Dragons*, Cersei I

---

moon tea were actually shown to have similar properties on regulating menstruation that modern birth control does in our world.

[4] Related to the trial situation, one theory that was debated in fandom after *A Feast for Crows* was whether Cersei may be pregnant from her affairs. Significance was placed on her gaining weight and the imagery and meaning of her finding a stillborn egg during breakfast. Followers of Maggy the Frog's prophecy were appeased with the possibility of the pregnancy being aborted or stillborn later on, while it was predicted to directly delay and affect the trial's verdict. However, this theory has been dealt a fatal blow by *A Dance with Dragons*, in particular by Cersei's naked walk of shame.

While the two upcoming trials run by the Faith emphasize the dangerous legal consequences of adultery, they also highlight that the married women of Westeros have developed clever ways to prevent their affairs from being discovered: careful timing, secrecy, and the use of contraceptives, like moon tea, which can prevent unexpected and unwanted pregnancies. There is another lioness in House Lannister who entered an arranged marriage like Cersei but who may have used such methods – along with her house's high standings – to escape the bounds of her marriage. Indeed, Cersei would have done well to have taken notes from her aunt, Genna Lannister. Both women have pressed against the bounds restricting their gender, in both the sexual realm and in their day-to-day behavior.     Genna, however, is generally wiser about it and acts a lot more like her brothers, Tywin and Kevan, than her niece.

Genna's personal conduct and demeaning attitude toward her husband, as well as her keeping of a personal singer that travels with her, are hints toward her possible infidelity.[5]   Jaime Lannister recounts his aunt's marriage situation in *A Feast for Crows*:

> *It was hard not to feel contemptuous of Emmon Frey.   He had arrived at Casterly Rock in his fourteenth year to wed a lioness half his age.   Tyrion used to say that Lord Tywin had given him a nervous belly for a wedding gift.   Genna has played her part, as well.   Jaime remembered many a feast where Emmon sat poking at his food sullenly whilst his wife made*

[5] Whitesmile Wat was one of Genna's personal singers who was brought with her to the siege of Riverrun.

*ribald jests with whatever household knight had been seated to her left, their conversations punctuated by loud bursts of laughter.* She gave Frey four sons, to be sure. *At least, she says they are his. No one in Casterly Rock had the courage to suggest otherwise, least of all Ser Emmon.*

*A Feast for Crows*, Jaime V

Genna certainly benefitted from the Lannisters' status as a great house. In a way, she outranks her husband from House Frey, which a young Tywin Lannister pointed out to Walder Frey's chagrin.[6] Having Tywin as an elder brother certainly helps when it comes to increasing one's status. This inherited imbalance and Ser Emmon's weasel-like personality differentiate this marriage from Cersei and Robert's relationship. However, Genna was wise enough to bear Emmon some sons, including their firstborn, Cleos, who has the distinctive Frey features. Cersei, on the other hand, was unwilling to give Robert even a single true heir. This refusal, as noted by Eddard Stark, increased the possibility of discovery as well as the potential consequences.

Genna may have allowed herself to have an illegitimate child of her own, in relation to her fourth son, Walder Frey, a 14-year-old page called "Red Walder" in the *Feast for Crows* appendix.[7] Why is he called *Red* Walder? Is it because he has red hair and, thus, earned the nickname, like Red Ronnet? Is it because he has the potentially recessive Lannister features, compared to the

---

[6] *A Feast for Crows.*

[7] Coined by our podcast as the Red Walder Hill theory, I came up with this interpretation while combing through the appendix one exciting afternoon.

other children with Frey genes and characteristics? In either case, perhaps the father was someone other than Ser Emmon? Or perhaps it has no special meaning, and Genna really did give her husband four legitimate sons. The point is that Red Walder would fit into a pattern of marital infidelity, and it would not be a surprise if he turned out to be an illegitimate child. The future interaction at Riverrun between Genna and Tom of Sevenstreams, the brotherhood with banners spy and singer who has fathered dozens of bastard children, will certainly be interesting![8]

Genna's elder brother, Tywin, has also faced the prospect of extramarital relationships, though, in his case, it is a question over his dwarf son, Tyrion Lannister. Tyrion noted that "all dwarves are bastards in their fathers' eyes," but, in this case, Tywin may actually have other reasons to suspect Tyrion's parentage. This idea falls into the general *Tyrion is a Targaryen* theory that has been debated around fandom for quite some time and was strengthened in some ways with the release of *A Dance with Dragons*.[9] The general idea is that Mad King Aerys raped Joanna Lannister and impregnated her, which she kept secret to protect Tywin's life, which would be in danger if he ever found out. Tywin himself had some unconfirmed doubts, revealing to Tyrion that he could not prove that he was not his.[10] If Tyrion were confirmed to be a Targaryen later in the series, this would be another example of

---

[8] Tom himself was once Lady Ravella Swan's lover.

[9] Tyrion's lack of Greyscale and Ser Barristan's mentioning of Aerys's troublesome behavior are a few examples of how *A Dance with Dragons* added to this theory.

[10] *A Storm of Swords*: "Men's laws give you the right to bear my name and display my colors, since I cannot prove that you are not mine."

adulterous relationships and their consequences being important to both Westerosi history and the overall plot of the *Ice and Fire* saga.

It is interesting to note that there is a more crackpot fan theory floating out there in relation to Tywin's children that says that Aerys was actually the father of Jaime and Cersei Lannister, the idea being some familial basis for the incest as well as some of Cersei's more harebrained actions and her particular enjoyment from the burning of the Tower of the Hand in *A Feast for Crows*.[11]  In addition, Jaime and Cersei could, as a matter of reproductive biology, have had different fathers.  Such a situation would have actually helped to dissuade Tywin from suspecting anything, since one of the children (Jaime) would have been his.  There is not much support for this theory, but it is worth mentioning to highlight the overall specter of infidelity that seems to be particularly attracted to the Lannisters.[12]

Opposing House Lannister in the game of thrones is House Stark, another family that has had recent forays into the realm of marital infidelity.  Eddard Stark, a man known to greatly value his personal honor, brought home a bastard son supposedly sired during the war, after his marriage to Catelyn Tully.  Through her description of Jon's upbringing, Catelyn highlights the societal norms in relation to male infidelity and to bastards.  Married men fathering bastards

---

[11] This was a theory favored by one of our past podcast hosts, Nancy.

[12] Lancel is another example of a Lannister intertwined with marital infidelity.  In this case, it is his wife from an unwanted marriage, Gatehouse Ami, who is likely to give him horns.  Lancel is unique among the Lannisters in accepting such infidelity — in fact, encouraging it, in a way — because he has decided to devote himself to the Seven.

is not unexpected, and even Catelyn herself was willing to accept that Ned strayed during the war. It was his unusual acceptance and close upbringing of Jon that irks Catelyn and provokes her taciturn treatment of him.

(Roose Bolton is brought up as a counter example, though he is probably still closer to the norm in relation to the treatment of bastards. Roose's illegitimate offspring, Ramsay, was the product of a nonconsensual form of extramarital relationship – specifically, Roose's (late) claiming of the first night with one of his smallfolk's new wives. Ramsay Bolton is a bastard obsessed with his illegitimate birth, and even a king's decree is not enough to soothe his insecurity. His quest for power leads him to possibly murder his half-brother, Dominic. Ramsay is the poster child of what can go wrong with bastard children in Westeros, the epitome of Catelyn's fears.)

Catelyn takes Jon Snow's presence to be a constant, irritating reminder of her husband's infidelity. Beyond her personal jealousy, she also worries about the implications in relation to inheritance, and she welcomes his decision to join the Night's Watch, ending that potential rival Snow bloodline. Catelyn warns her son Robb of the danger of legitimizing Jon, whose sons and grandsons could complicate future matters of succession.[13]

---

[13] An example of bastard blood having a consequence long down the line is Garth Greenhand's legendary sexual proclivity. Garth, the legendary first King of the Reach, liked to "plant his seed in fertile ground," and half the houses of the Reach can trace their descent back to him, at times complicating matters for House Tyrell. An example closer to the current timeline is the matter of the Hornwood succession considered by Bran and his advisors in *A Clash of Kings*, where Lord Hornwood's bastard was seriously

The best-known secret in the series, however, is that Jon is not Eddard's son, but, rather, the child of Rhaegar Targaryen and Lyanna Stark. This is perhaps the most famous of the fan theories, though there are arguments around the details: was it an abduction, a consensual affair, or a planned marriage? While Jon may be the product of their union, his legitimacy is still open to debate. Some fans have noted that the Targaryens have practiced legal polygamy in the past, and Elia of Dorne came from a family and land more tolerant toward diverse sexuality and relationships than most of Westeros. It is possible that Rhaegar married Lyanna and that Jon is one of his legitimate children, or that Jon may be an illegitimate child. In either case, Jon has already had an enormous impact on the series.

Prince Rhaegar was not the first Targaryen to potentially stray into infidelity, with serious consequences for the realm – as mentioned, King Aerys II may have fathered at least one of Tywin's children. Beyond that, infidelity was not only common in the Targaryen line, but a source of one of their greatest threats: the Blackfyres. Aegon IV, known as "Aegon the Unworthy," created the problem by siring many illegitimate children during his realm and compounded it by legitimizing them upon his death bed. The challenging of King Daeron II's rule by his half-brother Daemon Blackfyre and the struggle of the "Great Bastards" led to civil war on multiple occasions. In an attempt to bolster the Blackfyre claim to the throne, Daeron's own parentage was questioned during his rule. The whispers that Aemon the Dragonknight was his real father,

---

considered as a possible heir, over the possible objection of Lady Hornwood.

whether true or not, certainly had the potential to weaken Daeron's claim.

As Catelyn Stark noted, "the Blackfyre pretenders troubled the Targaryens for five generations, until Barristan the Bold slew the last of them on the Stepstones."[14]  The threat may have continued beyond that point, however.  One theory debated in fandom, particularly following *A Dance with Dragons*, is whether the Blackfyres may still be amongst us.  The theory is based on the fact that the Blackfyre line ended on the male side but may have produced further heirs on the female, including, potentially, the "Aegon" that was revealed in *Dance*.  The theory speculates that Aegon is a Blackfyre, potentially Illyrio's son, and that Varys himself is a Blackfyre, although these three different ideas aren't necessarily intertwined or reliant on each other.  The theory, if true, would explain why Varys might have helped to bring down the Targaryens, only to support them once again a short while afterwards – although there is much of Varys's behavior that would still need explaining.  This hypothesis would also be another example of an earlier infidelity and illegitimate child leading to serious and continuous consequences down the line.

Daemon Blackfyre was not the only one of Aegon the Unworthy's Great Bastards to leave a legacy that affects modern-day Westeros. Bittersteel's legacy was organizational rather than genetic, founding the Golden Company that has very recently invaded southern Westeros. Bloodraven himself is still around and potentially one of the most influential characters in the story. As such, Targaryen adultery and infidelity has had not only serious political consequences in

---

[14] *A Storm of Swords*.

Westeros, but it has also done much to develop and drive forward the plot of the series.

In relation to the plot, the five monarchs in the War of the Five Kings were impacted by marital infidelity, though in surprisingly different ways. Joffrey's roots to Cersei's incestuous affair are already clear. Robert's two brothers also were involved in marital infidelity. We can deduce that Renly and Loras continued their relationship after Renly's marriage, including the night before Renly's death. While Loras's support helped in securing the Tyrells in the first place, their continued affair, if Renly had lived, could have potentially undercut the Baratheon-Tyrell marriage alliance. It would have depended on how Margaery chose to deal with the situation and whether Renly would have successfully fathered some heirs. He believed he could do it, but his death, indirectly caused by Stannis's own infidelity, makes the situation moot.

Stannis Baratheon is intertwined with adultery in several different ways. He was not the first person to discover Cersei's affair, but he informed Jon Arryn of his suspicions and withdrew to Dragonstone, helping to set things in motion at the opening of *A Game of Thrones*. Stannis's accusations against Cersei were thrown back at him via Littlefinger's guile, with a questioning of the parentage of his own daughter, Shireen. While blatantly false, it had some effect and again highlights how even insinuations of infidelity are enough to cause insult and injury.

What is no longer an insinuation of infidelity, however, is Stannis's relationship with Melisandre. It was suspected for quite some time that Stannis was having an affair with the red priestess from Asshai; his distance from his own wife and his sharing of his tent were hints that set his own bannermen to talking. The shadow children birthed by Melisandre and matching Stannis's figure were further evidence of sexual relations, though the consent and consciousness involved has been debated. *A Dance with Dragons*'s subtle hint of her "little use[d]" bed in Stannis's absence reinforces the existence of the sexual nature of their relationship, and the significant impact that relationship has had on the overall narrative. It is even possible that Stannis's wife approves of the situation, given her religious fervor towards both Melisandre and R'hllor.

Unlike some of his rivals, the King in the North did not *technically* commit adultery, though, perhaps, it would have been better for him if he had. When Robb Stark spent the night with Jeyne Westerling, he was not married, but he was promised to wed another. He could have still gone through with the planned marriage and kept the Freys happy. Walder Frey, father of bastards himself, could hardly have complained even if Robb had fathered a bastard before marriage. It was Robb's decision to protect Jeyne's honor rather than the honor of the pact which led to serious – and fatal – complications shortly thereafter. It probably would have been better for him and his cause if he had acted more like his namesake and taken Jeyne as a mistress. However, that would not have been the Robb that Eddard Stark raised.

The last remaining king, Balon Greyjoy, took at least two salt wives in his youth but has not fathered any bastards that we know of. Again, perhaps it would have been better for him and for his cause if he had done so; Balon lost his two eldest male heirs in a failed rebellion, and his last remaining male successor became a ward and hostage of the enemy. He may have favored his daughter Asha after the rebellion, but this was an unstable succession position to leave the Iron

Islands in – particularly since his brother Euron was disgraced and in exile, Victarion lacked a wife and heir, and Aeron was quite likely abstinent due to his priesthood.   On the other hand, Roose Bolton warned that "boy lords are the bane of any house."[15]   There is no guarantee that another male heir would not have complicated things further, particularly if he became the puppet king of the wrong master.[16]

This review of marital infidelity has shown the wide impact it has had on Westerosi history (not to mention the plot of A Song of Ice and Fire), but it would be remiss not to consider the Dornish situation in greater depth and why unfaithfulness has not had a greater effect there. As noted by Martin himself, "blood, custom, geography, and history all helped to set the Dornishmen apart from the other kingdoms."[17] There are several distinctions in Dorne, both cultural and political, that alter the story there.

Queen Nymeria's continuing influence on Dorne is felt to this day.   The kingdom is less patriarchal than the rest of Westeros, and the weakening of patriarchy has naturally mitigated the impact of breaking the restraints of marriage. The equal primogeniture system can also undercut the effect of infidelity; the general rule of pregnancy in Westeros is that the mother of the child is always known, while the father, while assumed to be the husband, is not guaranteed. It is that uncertainty in succession that is threatened by marital infidelity and considered treasonous. Dorne has a higher percentage of female rulers and heirs compared to the rest of the kingdoms.

---

[15] A Dance with Dragons.
[16] Refer to A Podcast of Ice and Fire, episodes 68 and 69, for the offbeat Heir to the Iron Islands theory.
[17] A Dance with Dragons.

In these cases, the women may still give birth to bastards, but at least the succession would be equivalent to the male situation of fathering bastards elsewhere in Westeros – a blood connection would be maintained in inheritance.

Sexuality and sexual norms in Dorne are generally more relaxed and less repressive than the rest of Westeros, as well, which is noted in various songs and stories across the realm. Dornish peppers (and perhaps blood oranges) are thought to inflame Dornish passions and to make Dornish women wanton.[18] Bastards are better treated and have more opportunities for advancement. Prince Oberyn himself is rumored to have openly slept with both men and women and left behind a string of bastard daughters who exert considerable political influence and power. The Dornish way of life can bend the regular rules, norms, and consequences present in the rest of Westeros. Arianne Martell noted how her renowned uncle, Prince Lewyn, successfully kept a paramour, whereas other Kingsguard knights had been severely punished for breaking the vow of chastity and, essentially, their marriage to their sworn duty.[19] Ser Barristan the Bold also mentioned his sworn brother's paramour and acknowledged the different attitude toward sexuality present in Dorne.[20]

This whirlwind tour has reinforced the significant impact of marital infidelity in Westeros. It is not surprising that adultery has caught the eye of the fandom and that there are so many fan theories on it; instances of marital infidelity resonate in noble life and on those

---

[18] Refer to A Podcast of Ice and Fire, episode 68, for the Doran Martell Blood Oranges theory.

[19] *A Feast for Crows.*

[20] *A Dance with Dragons.*

playing the game of thrones.  Such instances are prime examples of what Martin often quotes as being the primary focus of storytelling, that of "the human heart in conflict with itself."[21]   It truly is the game of beds, with its fascinating middle grounds, that develops and propels much of Martin's *Song of Ice and Fire* saga.

---

[21] Martin makes this comment in most of his interviews.

# EVERY CASE IS DIFFERENT, EVERY CASE IS ALIKE

*Investigating murder investigations in Westeros*

John Jasmin

"Lysa says Jon Arryn was murdered." Only a sudden bolt of lightning or a tense chord from a pipe organ could have better underscored how dramatic that statement was when it was delivered early in *A Game of Thrones*. In case there was doubt, Catelyn Stark made clear that it was no casual accusation. Lysa had sent her a letter, penned in a secret language that only she would recognize and hidden in the false bottom of a wooden box. The box also contained a fine new lens, supposedly for Winterfell's observatory. Why a lens? "A lens is an instrument to help us see," Catelyn explained in all earnestness. With such deductive reasoning skills, it's no wonder that the mystery surrounding Jon Arryn's death not only went unsolved by House Stark, it was quickly forgotten. As it turns out, though, it is difficult to pursue justice in Westeros without an agency that can first pursue truth.

## The Case of Jon Arryn

Little is known about Jon Arryn's life. He was the Lord of the Eyrie and Warden of the East.

He fostered Eddard Stark and Robert Baratheon. He was the first to raise his banners in support of Robert's rebellion against Mad King Aerys. He married Lysa Tully and had with her a single, sickly son. He served as Hand of the King, essentially ruling Westeros while King Robert ate, drank, and wenched himself to an early grave. But it was Jon Arryn who died, suddenly and unexpectedly, at the start of the story. As Grand Maester Pycelle explained it, Jon had come to him one day "as hale and healthy as ever." The next morning, he was struck by a fever, too ill to leave his bed. A fortnight later, he was dead. Said Robert, "The sickness was like a fire in his gut. It burned right through him."

It's not surprising that Eddard was deeply affected by the news of Jon's death. Jon had been a father figure to him in the Eyrie, and later became a brother of sorts, too; each had wed a daughter of Hoster Tully. Perhaps it shouldn't be so surprising that Eddard, with Catelyn's urging, would feel the need to investigate Jon's death after Lysa made her bold accusation. Demanding answers to "why?" and "who is responsible?" would be a consistent reaction and a convenient excuse of someone still in the stages of grieving.

Of course, the same emotions that prevented Eddard from being rational about the Hand's death also precluded any chance that he would recuse himself as the chief investigator. The Stark way is the "older way," yes, but should the man who passes the sentence be the one who collects the evidence, too? Surely Eddard – the Lord of Winterfell, the Warden of the North, and now the Hand of the King – had enough responsibilities that this one, potentially important task could have been delegated to someone with both the time and the objectivity to see it done right. Ser Rodrik Cassel, Jory Cassel, or Maester Luwin, all of them trustworthy and capable servants of House Stark, would have been good choices here. Instead, Eddard went south to King's Landing himself.

The Hand of the King has legitimate duties that concern the well-being of the realm. Attempting to solve a mystery on the side can only distract from them. (Jon Arryn himself would probably attest to that!) The Hand must hold the king's court and rule with the king's voice, and he must do so while navigating all the political intrigues that pervade the capital. Here, Eddard struggled. However, he seemed to find success while playing detective, whereas it eluded him while playing the game of thrones. During his brief time in King's Landing, Ned figured out what it had taken Jon Arryn years to discover: Joffrey, Myrcella, and Tommen were not Robert's trueborn children. The heirs apparent to the Iron Throne were in fact the children born of an incestuous relationship between Queen Cersei Lannister and her twin brother, Ser Jaime.

In modern criminal law, convicting a person of murder is generally dependent on prosecutors providing three pieces of evidence: means, motive, and opportunity. Eddard did well to discern a motive for Cersei killing Jon Arryn, as it would be considered treason for the queen to commit adultery. To protect her own neck – as well as the fates of her unwitting children – Cersei would be highly motivated to prevent Jon from exposing her secret. On the other hand, Eddard merely assumed the means and opportunity of Cersei's crime. If Jon had been killed by poison, as Eddard suspected, Ned would need to identify the means (i.e., the poison) by which Jon died, and confirm the opportunity Cersei had to kill him. Because she was a queen and a wealthy Lannister, Eddard must have assumed that Cersei could easily acquire an undetectable poison. Similarly, the queen had free reign of the castle, so Eddard assumed she had plenty of chances to slip poison into the Hand of the King's food or wine goblet.   Having produced only a motive, Eddard failed to prove beyond reasonable doubt that Cersei was guilty of murdering Jon Arryn.

That was not the first time Eddard revealed his tendency to make faulty assumptions. Had he been more prudent from the start, he never would have assumed that Lord Arryn had been murdered in the first place.   Aside from Lysa's claim, there was not a single shred of evidence of murder.   Pycelle treated Jon in his final days and witnessed nothing unnatural.   He told Eddard, "I have seen more of illness than I care to remember, my lord.   I will tell you this: every case is different, and every case is alike. Lord Jon's death was no stranger than any other." It was Eddard, not Lysa, who suggested poison. Pycelle remained skeptical because there had been no telltale signs of it.   Regardless, Eddard persisted with his investigation.

Furthermore, Ned went to King's Landing with a prime suspect already in mind, even though Lysa made not just an unsubstantiated accusation, but an unspecified one, at that.   Who murdered Jon Arryn?   Lysa wrote in her cryptic letter, "The Lannisters.  The queen."  The latter could only be Cersei, but it's the former that should have troubled Eddard most.  Did Lysa mean to implicate all of House Lannister in Jon's murder?  If not, which of the many Lannisters were involved?  Was the queen the mastermind behind the conspiracy, or simply the agent that administered the killing blow?  Ned did not ask any of these questions (though, to be fair, he did raise other doubts) and targeted Cersei as the one to watch.   In his discussion with Pycelle about poison, Eddard clearly had her in mind. The grand maester called poison the weapon of choice for eunuchs (i.e., Varys). Again, Eddard dismissed this line of thought, assuming he had the correct suspect.

So when Eddard uncovered proof of Cersei's infidelity and treason, he was convinced that he had found the suspect for the crime, but he had instead found a crime for the suspect. He confronted Cersei in a memorable scene. "I know the truth Jon Arryn died for," Eddard told her. She unapologetically confessed to many of his accusations. Cersei did not, however, confess to killing Jon Arryn because, remarkably, Eddard never accused her of it. He linked Jon's death to Cersei's infidelity in his head, never once making the connection explicit to her. Cersei likely never realized that Eddard was in fact calling her a murderer, so she could not even deny it. She would have, though. An adulterer, yes. Jon Arryn's killer, no. Ultimately, Eddard went to his grave believing that he had solved the great mystery of his friend's death.

## The Cases of Kings

The people of Westeros are all too familiar with the Stranger, the aspect of their faith that represents death. "The Stranger was neither male nor female, yet both, ever the outcast, the wanderer from far places, less and more than human, unknown and unknowable." In Westeros, mother and child are fortunate to survive childbirth. Even then, they must stave off common diseases like greyscale and the bloody flux and hope that this is not the time for an epidemic like the Great Spring Sickness, which wiped out not only a king and his heirs, but tens of thousands of others, as well. A healthy man is not immune to a bar brawl blow or a desperate thief's dagger.   A fit man is exactly the type who is drafted into another man's war and killed for another's crown.  The manner of one's death may be unpredictable, but the Stranger comes for one and all.

So when does something as certain as taxes become a murder most foul?  Is an act of violence required before murder can be recognized?   In many civilizations, there are no more heinous crimes than the ones committed against the young and the innocent.  Consider how some children in Westeros died.  Sandor Clegane rode his horse down on a butcher's boy whose only sin was playing with Arya.  Raff the Sweetling drove a spear through Lommy Greenhand's throat when Lommy was too injured to walk without help.  And many of Robert Baratheon's bastard children were slaughtered, for fear that they might either discredit or challenge Joffrey's claim to the Iron Throne.  Despite these deplorable acts and the obvious guilt of those who perpetrated them, Sandor and Raff earned no reprisals.  Janos Slynt was banished to the Wall, but Cersei remained blameless, even though she ordered Slynt to hunt down Robert's bastards in the first place.  Clearly, violence alone is not a precursor to a call for justice.

Granted, these were lowborn children, so it shouldn't come as a surprise that they had few champions in death when they had none in life.  But what about the other end of the spectrum?  The knights of the Kingsguard were celebrated as the best swords in the realm, and each swore to protect his royal charge.  If a king could count on such an elite force to guard him, surely his life had value.  Surely his death would not be met by shrugs.

King Robert Baratheon was hunting in the Kingswood, possibly calculating which whorehouse to visit upon his return, when he was mortally wounded. He had drunk too much wine and missed his thrust against a boar. The beast subsequently ripped the king from groin to nipple with its tusks. No one would deny the boar's responsibility for Robert's demise, but the boar had some help. Ser Barristan Selmy and Renly Baratheon allowed Robert to face the boar alone, even though they knew he was too drunk to sit his saddle. Lancel Lannister made sure Robert stayed drunk, keeping his wineskin ever filled. And none of this accounted for the potential of active foul play. Varys would later muse, "If the boar had not done for Robert, it would have been a fall from a horse, the bite of a wood adder, an arrow gone astray... the forest is the abattoir of the gods."

King Renly Baratheon was arming for battle, possibly considering if an antlered helm might be too indecorous, when a shadow slipped into his tent and plunged a blade through his gorget. Brienne of Tarth and Catelyn Stark became the prime suspects among a number of other rumors spread by the smallfolk, some more fantastic than others. In truth, the shadow assassin had been conjured by the red witch Melisandre, at Stannis Baratheon's command. But with the deed done and Renly's army disbanded, the actual identity of Renly's killer mattered little. Ser Loras Tyrell eventually discharged Brienne of any wrongdoing. He would not pursue the mystery further.

King Balon Greyjoy was crossing a bridge that connected his castles at Pyke, possibly making a round trip because he forgot to reap in one what he sowed in the other, when a stiff wind blew him off the bridge and dashed him upon the rocks below. Accidents happen, of course, but what made Balon's death so mysterious was the timely reappearance of his brother Euron Crow's Eye. After two years in exile, Euron returned to the Iron Islands a day after Balon died and claimed the castle and crown by rights. A kingsmoot would settle the matter of succession in Euron's favor. Few would raise any suspicion about Balon's death after that.

King Robb Stark was enjoying his uncle's wedding, possibly thinking of some bawdy joke to deliver during his toast, when the wedding turned red from his own blood. He was betrayed by his bannermen. Lord Walder Frey conspired with Houses Lannister and Westerling to bring about Robb's downfall. Lord Roose Bolton personally twisted his sword into Robb's heart. Walder and Roose happily accepted lands and titles as rewards for their misdeeds, all but admitting to the crime of regicide. Nevertheless, none of Robb's allies demanded vengeance for their fallen king. The North remembers, perhaps, but the North has yet to remember more than how to nurse its grudges.

King Joffrey Baratheon was admiring the pigeon pie at his own wedding feast, possibly wondering if baking pigeons was just as fun as shooting them with a crossbow, when he choked to death. In his final moments, Joffrey had clawed at his throat, desperate for air. Or was he poisoned? No sooner had Cersei let go of Joffrey's lifeless body than she accused Tyrion of her son's murder. Tyrion was arrested, tried, and convicted, although Littlefinger would later admit to Sansa that Tyrion was innocent; Littlefinger himself claimed responsibility for poisoning Joffrey, with an assist from Lady Olenna Tyrell.

None of the kings expected to die the day they did. Their lives were cut short, far from the ideal of succumbing to old age, surrounded by hundreds of fat grandchildren, with a woman to tend to their final wishes. Instead, the kings died under curious circumstances, if not overt sabotage. Robert and Balon's deaths were convenient, Renly's was bizarre, and Robb's was brazen. Yet none of those four resulted in an investigation or a trial, however perfunctory. Only Joffrey's death was exposed to scrutiny. But why? There was no more evidence of murder in Joffrey's case than there was with any of the other kings; there was no evidence of poison whatsoever. The only thing that made Joffrey's death different from the others was that someone actually demanded a trial over it.

### Case Closed?

Catelyn Stark could be forgiven for abandoning pursuit of Jon Arryn's killer; it was hardly a priority after Eddard was executed and Robb began his rebellion. She would never learn that it was actually Lysa who had, in fact, poisoned Jon. Apparently the secret language that the two sisters had contrived as little girls was complex enough to be able to say, "Jon Arryn was murdered," but it had no words for, "And I done it!" Similarly, Cersei Lannister could be forgiven for believing Joffrey's case closed; even though Littlefinger was responsible for the death, Tyrion would be the one tried and found guilty. No one else, however, seemed bothered by the fact that these two cases – like so many others in Westeros – may have been improperly resolved.

The cases of Jon Arryn and Joffrey Baratheon share three traits that may help explain why so many murders in Westeros go unsolved. First, the cases were largely dependent on someone making a firm accusation of crime.

Criminologists refer to the number of unreported crimes as "the dark figure." Westeros's dark figure must be dark as night, if our cases are representative. Without Lysa naming Jon's death a murder, there would have been no investigation. Without Cersei blaming Tyrion for her son's death, there would have been no trial.

Secondly, the cases were poorly investigated. Eddard made too many faulty assumptions, failed to collect the proper evidence, and targeted the wrong culprit. Cersei similarly prejudged Tyrion's guilt. She presented witnesses who could speak of his immoral character, but none who could actually confirm an act of murder.

Finally, and perhaps most significantly, neither Eddard nor Cersei should have led their respective investigations in the first place, given their personal connections to the victims. That responsibility should have fallen to a third party, one that could act on their behalf and still seek the truth without bias. Of course, such an agency does not yet exist in Westeros. Trials by combat are used instead to determine the guilt of the defendant in the sight of gods and men. As Tyrion might tell you, this system is flawed. While the gods may indeed favor the innocent, the weaknesses of man always intervene. Bronn won Tyrion's first trial by exploiting the chivalry of his opponent. Oberyn Martell lost Tyrion's second trial by letting his own vengeance overcome him. It didn't matter that Tyrion was innocent in either instance; he walked free in one and was condemned in the other.

The legal system in *A Song of Ice and Fire* matches the time it is supposed to be set in, before police and lawyers, before due process, before justice is blind. But the story's emphasis on murder mysteries and the failure to solve them says as much about the imperfection of man as it does about the world men inhabit.  Justice is not possible without truth, and truth is subject to man's variable roles and interpretations.  For a murder to be resolved properly, someone must first realize that a crime has been committed, someone must investigate it, and someone must then rule on the evidence.  Throughout all that, they must never allow their emotions, biases, loyalties, and obligations to affect their judgment. What an unfeasible task, especially in a world without codified laws to guide them.   It's no wonder that when a series of mysterious deaths occurred in Harrenhal and again in Winterfell, people found it easier to believe that ghosts were responsible rather than to pursue the truth.

# YOU WIN OR YOU SIT THE BENCH

*Power ranking – NFL style – the top players in the game of thrones*

Douglas Cohen

When I was first approached to contribute an essay to this project from a fan's perspective, my initial thought was, "What is there to say about this series that the fans haven't said a million times over?" Still, having been on the George R.R. Martin bandwagon since before the bandwagon even existed, I was intrigued at the prospect of making a contribution dealing with my favorite series of books. So I decided to let this invitation roll around in my subconscious for a while and see if anything grabbed me. With this sort of wait-and-see attitude, imagine my surprise when an idea took hold that very same day.

As many of George's fans are aware, the man is a massive fan of the NFL. As it happens, so am I. So it struck me as being some good fan-inspired fun if, in honor of George's love for football, I offered up some power rankings concerning the top players of the game of thrones. While this is far from a traditional essay, I think it's fair to say that power ranking the characters according to their deviousness and political wheeling-and-dealing certainly captures the spirit of this project, and if that's good enough for the editor, it's good enough for me.

Of course, not everyone reading this essay is necessarily familiar with the idea of power rankings, so for those not inclined toward following the NFL or other team sports on a professional or collegiate level, allow me to provide a brief explanation about them while doing my best to keep your eyes from rolling back into your skull with boredom.

Power rankings are bogus. You can find them employed for almost any team sport, but they're particularly popular for the NFL. Basically, the people writing for various sports blogs, websites, and other media outlets rank the teams from first to worst (or vise versa). In the NFL, where each team plays once a week, revised power rankings are put out with the conclusion of each week's games. With actual league standings, it all comes down to records and various tiebreakers. Power rankings are much more opinion-based. There is no exact formula. The experts (and in many cases, I use that term loosely) compiling these rankings look at records and tiebreakers, but they also consider injuries, a team's potential, winning and losing streaks, etc. all to determine which team is the best at that point in the season. As I said, it's all bogus.

But it's also good fun. Power rankings inspire a good deal of debate and discussion among sports fans, something fans of George's books know about all too well. So when this idea struck me, I became rather excited. A quick internet search revealed there was one online newspaper already doing week-to-week power rankings for the HBO series, and the editor informed me the Tower of the Hand website was also doing such rankings. As I mentioned already, I didn't want to retread something that's been discussed a million times already, but my idea was to power rank the characters according to the books, not *Game of Thrones*. Additionally, the television series is only two seasons in, which means I'm feeling plenty comfortable about offering my bogus rankings and getting my geek on. Given that George's fans are legion, it's entirely possible someone somewhere has already done something like this, but if so, I am satisfied to live in my bubble and believe otherwise.

So with this said, I now present to you my power rankings for the top 10 players of the game of thrones as of the conclusion of *A Dance with Dragons.* Please note that my list will only account for characters that are still *definitively* alive. For dramatic anticipation, I've chosen to deliver this list from worst to first. So sit back and consider the rankings, and afterward go ahead and discuss, debate, disagree... and most of all, please enjoy.

10. *Roose Bolton:* Soft-spoken and coldblooded as a reptile, Roose Bolton excels when it comes to cunning and betrayal. A key player in the events of the Red Wedding, he succeeded with his co-conspirators in toppling House Stark. In switching sides and going over to the Lannisters, Roose gained himself a rich and powerful ally while being raised to Warden of the North. By marrying the fattest daughter of Lord Walder Frey, Roose also secured himself a powerful ally in the Riverlands, giving his coffers an ample boost in the process. The North remembers, though, and Roose understands this all too well, which is why he made certain to secure himself such powerful new friends before turning his cloak.

Caution has been the key to Roose's advancement, and while his ambitions have stopped short of the Iron Throne by all appearances, he has still reached too far. With a few notable exceptions, his countrymen want his head on a platter and are already plotting against him. At the same time, the North continues getting ripped apart with incessant wars instead of preparing for winter, and Roose will not be able to count on his allies to the south for food or support once winter hits. On top of this, his sole successor is Ramsay Bolton, who killed Roose's legitimate heir and threatens to destroy the fortunes of his lord father's entire house in his animal lust for power and dominion over everyone and everything around him. Perhaps Roose would be better served getting his own house in order instead of worrying about the Starks and others.

9. *Olenna Tyrell:* Shrewd with her decisions and sharp with her tongue, the Queen of Thorns brings a wealth of wisdom and experience to the game of thrones, all in the guise of a harmless old grandmother. She is not the official leader of House Tyrell, and her advancing age places certain physical limitations on her, but she is quick to perceive the truth of almost any given situation – more so than the rest of her ambitious house – which gives her a marked edge when it comes to making wise decisions. As the elder Tyrell and mother to her house's lord, she still wields enough influence that she can often make her son, Mace Tyrell, take actions or make requests to her house's benefit, whether it is through blunt words or subtle steering. She is also clever enough to make use of her frailties, for it was the harmless old grandmother guise that allowed her to get close enough to Joffrey Baratheon to bring him down with no one casting a suspicious eye her way.

Unfortunately, her son Mace is something of an oaf, which can limit Olenna's effectiveness. It is no doubt a source of constant frustration for her that the Tyrells wield so much power but often fail to employ it properly. She does what she can to keep them in the game by maximizing every ounce of intelligence and cunning she can muster, but with the Lannister alliance unraveling, their longtime enemies from Dorne stirring along their southern borders, the Golden Company on their eastern borders, and the Iron Islanders harrying their western shores, the Tyrells are surrounded by enemies. By all appearances, they are a rose about to wilt. It seems that Olenna should have grown a couple of extra thorns to keep her son's ambitions in check.

8. *Euron Greyjoy:* In some ways, the Crow's Eye is the most dangerous player of all, because he is unquestionably insane. Much like the Joker in Gotham City, he is a wild card that must be accounted for, someone capable of wreaking havoc on unexpected levels. You can strategize on the battlefield, and you can scheme and plot in the game of thrones, but it all goes out the window when trying to plan against an unhinged mind.

Lunacy aside, he is also a pirate captain of the highest caliber. He employs wizards to provide his ship favorable winds. He braved the ruins of old Valyria and discovered the dragon horn, one of the ultimate game changers in the entire story. Such daring – along with an understanding of his people's nature – led to him trumping his brother's claim to the Seastone Chair at the Kingsmoot. He proved his understanding for politics when he decreed his niece Asha would be wed to Erik Anvil-Breaker, negating one of his chief rivals and turning the other one into a staunch supporter. And he made certain to hold onto the loyalties of his newfound subjects by promising them what they love most: pillage and plunder.

Euron's lunacy is a double-edged sword, though. Daring to attack the Tyrells before the dragons are in his possession is a madman's gambit, especially with the Iron Fleet abroad. For now, the element of surprise is on his side, but it won't last with the Redwyne fleet bearing down. Euron also made the critical mistake of sending his brother Victarion off with the dragon horn to bring him back a dragon and a Targaryen wife. While wedding the last Targaryen would further solidify Euron's play for the Iron Throne, he has severely underestimated his brother's pliability. He offered Victarion the Seastone Chair, but it won't be enough.

So while his madness helped steer him into excellent position, this same madness threatens to cost him everything, for a saner man would have hesitated to trust Victarion after the way Euron wronged him in the past. Even so, Euron must not be wholly discounted from the game of thrones. When he learns of his brother's betrayal, his wrath will be righteous, and he will surely have a final gambit to play (perhaps whatever lurks beneath his eye patch)... but because he's insane, there is no telling what it might be. We also must not discount the possibility that everything Euron has done is not the product of his insanity, but part of a grander plan that has yet to be revealed. Without question, the Crow's Eye is dangerous, but at the moment, we can only rank him according to what we know for certain, which is that his insanity appears to be threatening all of his accomplishments.

7. *Melisandre:* Minion of the Lord of Light, wielder of flame and shadow, the red priestess commands great power in the service of R'hllor as

she plays kingmaker and prepares for the final battle against the forces of the Other. She has chosen to support Stannis Baratheon's claim to the Iron Throne, and, depending on how much credence one lends to her magical powers, she has had a hand in the deaths of up to four of his rival kings:    Renly Baratheon, Balon Greyjoy, Robb Stark, and Joffrey Baratheon. She also helped bring down Storm's End – one of the most impregnable fortresses in Westeros – and in Mance Rayder, the King-beyond-the-Wall, she has bound a fifth king to her righteous will. With a better understanding than most about what is at stake, each of her actions takes on additional significance as she seeks to control and steer Stannis to glorious victory. To date, there is no one else quite so skilled at either felling men of power or bending them to her will.

But despite such impressive powers and achievements, she is doomed to remain in the lower portion of the rankings because of her failure to properly interpret signs and prophecies. She believes Stannis Baratheon to be Azor Ahai reborn, the figure to lead the forces of the Lord of Light against those of the Other. While debate rages concerning who Azor Ahai reborn really is (Jon Snow!), enough clues have been dropped to conclude it's not Stannis; in other words, Melisandre is pursuing a dead end. She may be powerful and she may be influencing the course of events, but until she discovers the truth, her agenda will not receive as much respect in the power rankings as many of those who are effectively pursuing their endgames.

6. *Moqorro:* Another priest in service to the Lord of Light and the story's newest character to grace the rankings, he has the most potential to move up or down in the rankings because much

about him still remains a mystery. What we do know is the following: based on the small sample size we've read, he is more skilled at reading the future than his fellow red priest, Melisandre. And in becoming the most trusted advisor to Victarion Greyjoy – the fiercest pirate captain in the Iron Isles – he now has access to the Iron Fleet, the strongest part of the Ironborn's considerable naval power. Even more importantly, he now has a pipeline to the dragon horn from old Valyria, which can give a man control over dragons. As Victarion's fleet will soon reach Meereen and two of Daenerys Targaryen's dragons are currently in the city, there is a very real chance that when all is said and done, this priest of fire will have access to a dragon or two through Victarion. In a very short time, Moqorro has put himself in position to capitalize upon some excellent opportunities.

To date, he has made no mistakes in the game of thrones, and while the moves he's made are limited, they're also impressive. But until his plans become clearer and can be better assessed, he remains relegated to the bottom half of the power rankings.

5. *Doran Martell:*   The Prince of Dorne, aye... and also the Prince of Patience. For almost 20 years, he has been waiting for his vengeance to unfold. Such extreme patience has certain benefits. Other players have been tipping their hands first, which often results in them making mistakes first. Houses Lannister and Tyrell – the two families Doran and his kingdom have the most cause to hate – are committing forces and wealth against other foes and spreading themselves ever thinner, while the nation of Dorne has remained relatively unscathed.

Doran has also forged significant alliances with Varys the Spider and Illyrio Mopatis, two of the most connected players in the game of thrones. The sudden appearance of the Golden Company upon the shores of Westeros will unquestionably force Doran to make some decisions before he's ready, but the upside is that Dorne can easily make common cause with the most dangerous mercenary company in the world, and with the Tyrells distracted by the Iron Islanders and their alliance with the Lannisters steadily fraying, Doran is in a position to be one of those dictating events as the fate of Westeros comes to a head. And if things should go awry, Dorne remains well protected thanks to its geography, not to mention that the kingdom should be the last place on the continent that must deal with the Others. Last but not least, now that everyone in Doran's family is on the same page regarding his plans, he also has the Sand Snakes – trained at the knee of the great Oberyn Martell himself – to carry out his will.

Of course, it's not all sunshine. Doran himself is bound to a wheelchair and cannot be the commanding physical leader his brother Oberyn was, the kind of leader the people of Dorne would much prefer. And the whole matter of patience is not without cost; when you wait so long, something is bound to go wrong. In this case, Khal Drogo's infamous pot of gold destroyed the arranged marriage between Viserys and his daughter, Arianne; Daenerys Targaryen is no longer under the hold of Illyrio and proved less than willing to marry Quentyn Martell; Doran's brother and son are both dead, whittling down the members of House Martell significantly; and assuming Daenerys eventually reaches Westeros and does not make common cause with Aegon,

House Martell will be faced with the decision of which Targaryen to declare for.

Doran's house is primed to achieve its long-sought vengeance and could marry back into the Iron Throne when all is said and done, but Doran's entire existence since Robert Baratheon's ascension to the Iron Throne has been predicated around waiting. Each move has been chosen with the utmost care. With everything coming to a boil, he must demonstrate he's capable of changing tactics and making quick and decisive decisions if he wishes to win the game of thrones and see House Martell achieve both vengeance and survival.

4. *Tyrion Lannister:* No one on this list has experienced the constant highs and lows of the game of thrones firsthand like Tyrion Lannister. He has risen as high as the Hand of the King and fallen as low as a slave in a strange land with a bounty on his head, courtesy of his sister, Cersei. But regardless of his situation (and when he's not drinking himself into oblivion), his mind is always at work, seeking to turn every situation to his advantage.

His capacity for survival, scheming, planning, and deduction are off the charts. To cite a few examples: surviving the Vale of Arryn; negating Janos Slynt, outwitting Grand Maester Pycelle and uncovering his role in Jon Arryn's death, keeping the entire small council guessing and off-balance, and fortifying King's Landing against invasion while serving as Hand; figuring out Joffrey Baratheon was behind the attempt on Bran Stark's life; uncovering the identity of Aegon Targaryen and leveraging this into winning the trust of Aegon's caretakers; and not only escaping slavery, but gaining the protection of the mercenary group the Second Sons.

Despite his noble lineage, he is constantly looked down upon for being a dwarf.  Combined with his ugliness, it has placed certain limitations on his effectiveness, which makes his achievements that much more impressive.

Of course, Tyrion's physical stature is not his only limitation.  He is too sharp-tongued for his own good, and while he is capable of making cutthroat decisions, in his heart of hearts, he is a romantic.  It clouds his thought process and often leads to emotional decisions that are not in his best interests.  He spends too much time drinking to escape his pain, and his physical deformities have led to a deep level of self-consciousness that he tries to compensate for with his intellect and his acerbic tongue.

Given the scorn he suffers at the hands of his own family, the aristocracy at large, and almost everyone else, it's difficult to fault Tyrion his weaknesses.  And no matter how many times he gets knocked down, he perseveres.  While he may not be tops on this list, when the chips are down, Tyrion Lannister is not someone to bet against.  And when the story reaches its conclusion, I'll bet on him becoming the new Lord of Casterly Rock.

3. *Varys the Spider/Illyrio Mopatis:*  With their plans and machinations so intertwined, these two peas in a pod share the number three slot as we examine the top three spots in the power rankings.  While there are still some unanswered questions regarding this pair, their plans are finally taking shape.  They have a lot going for them:  money, power, spies, armies, and loads upon loads of secrets.  The two of them have been masterful in orchestrating events on both sides of the narrow sea.

In Westeros, Varys has been privy to the realm's most important secrets as a member of the small council, and what he doesn't learn on the council, his "little birds" report back to him. With so much information at his fingertips, he has always known exactly how much information to feed each and every person, in order to keep their trust, keep them off-balance, or keep them in fear. Whether he is coercing Ned Stark to swallow his precious honor, unearthing secrets about the most powerful families in Westeros, spiriting Tyrion overseas to save him from certain execution, or slaying Maester Pycelle and Kevan Lannister to ensure the end of the Lannister-Tyrell alliance, the Spider is always weaving plans within plans in his master web. Combined with the limitless funds of Illyrio Mopatis at his disposal, Varys has proven himself one of the more flexible players in the game of thrones. Even when it seems as if he's serving the will of others, he is spinning his own web and turning matters to his own advantage.

And while Varys has been steadily undermining the political power base in King's Landing, over in Essos, Illyrio Mopatis has been harboring the world's greatest secret in the form of Aegon Targaryen and has been nurturing Targaryen armies to conquer Westeros after the Iron Throne has spent the better part of its power fighting foes on its own shores. With the armies of Dorne waiting in the south to provide further support to these Targaryen saviors, Varys and Illyrio would seem to be in excellent position to come out on top.

The problem is some of the other players are crimping their style. Petyr Baelish manipulated events to cause the Starks and the Lannisters to go to war before Varys and Illyrio wanted them to. Daenerys's beloved Khal Drogo destroyed the arranged marriage between Viserys and Princess Arianne of Dorne that they had a hand in brokering. On top of this, after Khal Drogo died and Daenerys used the wealth on Illyrio's ship to help build an empire of her own, they lost whatever hold they had over Daenerys and her armies. To compound matters, they have severely underestimated Tyrion's skills of deduction, for he has discovered the truth about Aegon Targaryen, and Aegon himself has gone rogue, taking the armies of the Golden Company overseas before anyone else wished to do this.

But despite the unforeseen circumstances, Varys and Illyrio should still be moving and shaking in the game for a long while yet. Aegon may have gone overseas without their consent, but he still considers them an ally. Dorne does, as well, and Daenerys should still have a soft spot toward Illyrio for brokering the marriage to Khal Drogo, her sun and stars. With much of Westeros in shambles, they are poised to capitalize and return the Targaryens to the throne. And let's not forget these two excel at keeping secrets... chances are they're still holding on to a few more with the endgame approaching.

2. *Petyr Baelish:* Does anyone enjoy the game of thrones as much as Petyr Baelish? His roots belong to the lowliest of noble houses, but thanks to his scheming, backstabbing, alliances, seductions, and, of course, his notoriously deep pockets, Littlefinger is now one of the most powerful men in Westeros. Official titles aside, he has the Riverlands and the Vale in his pocket, the armies of the Vale are unscathed, and he is living in the Eyrie, another of Westeros's more impregnable fortresses. On top of this, he currently remains in the good graces of both the Lannisters and the Tyrells, and as long as he has

Sansa Stark in his clutches, he is poised to make a play to take over the North. That would give him three of the Seven Kingdoms. There is no question that Petyr Baelish wants the Iron Throne, but his path is a circuitous one. He means to control as much of the Seven Kingdoms as possible before he makes his true intentions known.

And this is indeed the way of Littlefinger. He has been manipulating his way to greater and greater power ever since he seduced Lysa Arryn, which he used to gain a foothold in King's Landing. From there, everything has basically gone according to plan. When roadblocks like Tyrion Lannister got in his way – promising him Harrenhal only to pull the football away, ala Lucy to Charlie Brown – Littlefinger still managed to get his way in the end. He even found a younger, prettier replacement for his beloved Catelyn Stark in her daughter, Sansa, because regardless of his designs to marry her off to Harry the Heir, I hold no doubts that Petyr means to have Sansa for himself. But that will probably happen after their marriage seals her (and by shadowy extension, his) claim over the North. The plans of Littlefinger are never simple or direct, but with his fingerprints on them, they're almost always effective.

But even the best of them make mistakes. Unbeknown to Petyr, there is a traitor in his household. Toward the end of *A Feast for Crows*, we learn that Lord Baelish has hired some new soldiers to augment his household. Read the introductions of these soldiers carefully, and you'll notice one of them is the Mad Mouse, the hedge knight who was traveling with Brienne earlier in the book, looking to find Sansa Stark and collect the reward for returning her to the Iron Throne. Littlefinger is getting sloppy, because he failed to vet these men properly. While it's doubtful the Mad Mouse will kill Littlefinger, there will clearly be fallout from this blunder. It is a small chink in Littlefinger's armor – the only one he's revealed to date – but it may be a sign of things to come. And unless he succeeds in seducing Sansa, at some point the student may school the teacher.

1. *Daenerys Targaryen:*    She may have nobler lineage than Petyr Baelish, but considering their situations at the beginning of the story, her rise to power came from a lower place. From being little more than the child-wife to a dangerous barbarian whose sole purpose was to provide her intimidating husband physical pleasure, she became a *khaleesi* in deed as well as title.    From here she became the Mother of Dragons... and let's face it, dragons are the ultimate game changer.    Her successful hatching of the dragons also led to her becoming the first woman to lead her own *khalasar*.

But this was just the opening act.    Since then, she has systematically built her empire with guile, intelligence, force, threats, money, charisma, and beauty.    She has overthrown three separate cities in Astapor, Yunkai, and Meereen, becoming the most powerful force in Slaver's Bay in the process.    And not only did she bring dragons back to the world, she has also successfully tamed one of them, making it servile to her.    Since the dragon is large enough to ride, she is now an army unto herself.    And while she has been forced to flee Meereen due to potential betrayals, Ser Barristan Selmy is minding her interests in her absence, and the end of *A Dance with Dragons* leaves her poised to take over at least part of the Dothraki hordes – the finest horsemen in the world – and add them to her existing armies. Take her dragon, her forces in Meereen, and these Dothraki hordes, and Daenerys Targaryen is on the verge of assembling the most dangerous fighting force in the world.

Of course, even the top player in the game of thrones is fallible. As fierce as Daenerys is, she is letting emotion get in the way of her ultimate goals. Her feelings for Daario Naheris are clouding her judgment, and while her decision to abolish the slave trade is admirable, it is not something that is advancing her power in Slaver's Bay or her goal of reclaiming the Iron Throne; it is a decision of the heart, based on her past. Her court is also rife with traitors, making it difficult to trust many of her advisors.

Overall, she has made more mistakes than Petyr Baelish and has more enemies to deal with – ones she knows of, ones she suspects, and ones she has no idea about – but many of these enemies are due to her dragons. As has already been noted, the dragons are game changers, and she has tamed one of them already. Domesticating Drogon negates a good deal of her mistakes. Fire destroys, but a blacksmith will tell you it also creates, and Daenerys is about to do both. She will burn her enemies with dragon fire, and that same flame will forge an army not seen since dragons went out of the world. While it's true that Victarion is coming with the dragon horn, Daenerys is also away from the city – so for now, she and her dragon will remain beyond his clutches.

And as long as Drogon remains under her control and the other dragons are without masters, Daenerys Targaryen can advance her goals better than anyone else. And this is the essence of the game of thrones: achieving your aims through whatever means necessary as you strive toward greater and greater power. No one has done this more, done it better, or is better equipped to continue doing this than Dany. When she reaches Westeros, she will have choices to make regarding Dorne and Aegon, and her dragons will be needed to deal with the Others – but those are concerns for future books.

For now, based on events to date, I proclaim Daenerys Targaryen the Queen of the Game of Thrones.

### Players to Watch

And as a special bonus, here are three players to watch going forward.  Based on what they do in the next book, players two and three both have a very real chance of cracking the top ten come the end of *The Winds of Winter*:

1. *Cersei Lannister:*  While she excels at screwing everything up, she also has a gift for survival and remaining relevant.  With Kevan Lannister's death and a reanimated Gregor Clegane to serve as her champion, she is poised to once again dictate policy from the Iron Throne... for the moment, anyway.

2. *Jaqen H'ghar:*  His goals remain mysterious, but he has situated himself in the Citadel, posing as Pate the pig boy.  Whatever he's planning, it's big, and with all the skills he has at his disposal, the possibilities are endless.

3. *Sansa Stark:*  She is learning the game of thrones from one of the masters.  At some point, expect her to become more assertive as she puts into play what she has learned.

### Honorable Mention

He's dead and therefore ineligible to make the list, but if I'm discussing the best players of the game of thrones, I need to at least give a brief tip of the cap to *Tywin Lannister*. His accomplishments in this field matched up with the best of them, and were he still alive, he would surely rank among the top players. In post-Targaryen Westeros, he was without question the most powerful man on the continent.

Much of what his son Tyrion knows about the game is thanks to his dead sire, and since Tyrion's adeptness at the game of thrones has saved his life against all odds on numerous occasions, it only adds to the irony that he killed his father. Somewhere in the seven hells, this knowledge is surely making Tywin Lannister frown over steepled fingers.

# THE NARRATIVES OF WINTER

*Discerning the structure of Martin's saga and
teasing out its final act*

Marc N. Kleinhenz

To understand something, a wise man once
said, you must know its origins. In terms of
storytelling, this is invariably true, but a strong –
and, perhaps, more important – corollary would
have to be something even simpler: to understand
a narrative, you must know its structure.

It's almost deceptively easy, right? A
tautology wrapped in CliffsNotes, which is
especially offensive to a story as convoluted as
George R.R. Martin's *A Song of Ice and Fire*. It is
still, however, true, as is evidenced by a
particularly vivid memory from my junior year of
high school. We were reading Robert M. Pirsig's
*Zen and the Art of Motorcycle Maintenance* in our
English class, and I was one of the few, thanks to
my interest in philosophy and the fact that I had
cheated and read the novel already, that actually
had a fairly loose grasp of the material (hey, to a
17-year-old, Pirsig's rather rudimentary survey of
Western philosophical history is overwhelmingly,
well, overwhelming).

When attempting to explain *Zen* to a
befuddled friend the night before a test, I found
myself backpedaling – not unlike the narrator of
the book itself – to the point that I simply had to

explain what the story itself was on a fundamental level. "It's about a guy riding his motorcycle with his son and buddies, and, along the way, he has a series of discussions with himself, starting with philosophy but ending with his life story. Oh, and there's some motorcycle maintenance, too." A light bulb went off over my buddy's head and suddenly the whole thing just *clicked* into place for him (though I think he still failed that test).

It's the structure, stupid. Pragmatism may be the basest level of human knowledge or existence, but one can't get very far without it (trust me: I've tried). The same is true in the literary sense, where understanding the framework an author is working within suddenly opens up the entire narrative panorama. And, as an added bonus, once this storytelling DNA has been cracked, the tale's ending is usually laid pretty bare; the genetic strands of one's beginning oftentimes spell out his death, after all.

And (*The Winds of*) *Winter is* coming.

### In the Beginning

At the very earliest stage, when Martin was hurriedly scribbling down chapters about derelict brothers getting their heads chopped off and direwolf pups being discovered off the side of the road without any real sense of what was coming afterwards, the entirety of *A Song of Ice and Fire* was just one, extremely large, novel. This must have lasted for all of five minutes, however – just as much time as was needed to fill out the story's burgeoning outline. Once compiled, it was pretty clear to George that he had a series on his hands (publishers absolutely refuse to release books that are over a certain page count, thanks to the overcrowded nature of bookshelves and the demands of retailers), and he settled on the traditional trilogy: *A Game of Thrones, A Dance with Dragons,* and *The Winds of Winter.*

The wonderfully straightforward element of trilogies is their de facto acquiescence with the three-act structure of storytelling, a narrative construct that is most prolific in Hollywood (where Martin spent a decent chunk of his writing career). The first installment is the introduction; the second, the rising action; the third, the climax and resolution. (Think of any [good] modern film trilogy, such as the ever-popular *Star Wars* or the deliciously dense *Matrix* series, for a pretty good example of how the three-act model works.) In Martin's original conceptualization, each novel/act would have been 800 pages in length, resulting in a story that would ultimately have been twice as large as J.R.R. Tolkien's *Lord of the Rings* trilogy.

It, of course, was not meant to be. To make a byzantine story (of a byzantine story) as concise as possible, when George reached and then exceeded the 800-page mark of *Game,* he was only roughly one-third of the way through where he expected to be, necessitating that book's being divided up into its own trilogy (whose last installment, *A Storm of Swords,* would, by itself, be longer than *The Lord of the Rings,* incidentally). Seeing that the overstuffed outline for his first projected novel was so problematic, and seeing that *Winds of Winter*'s planned contents were similarly bulging against their restraints, George decided to save himself a lot of advance grief and split that one into multiple books, as well – though, this time, it was just two (*The Winds of Winter* and *A Time for Wolves*), and not three. *Dance* looked like a safe bet to remain one single novel, he thought, so he left that alone – until he tried to actually write the damn thing and was forced, ultimately, to likewise cleave that one in two, with *A Feast for Crows* being the new entry.

(The fact that Martin tried his damnedest to ensure that *Dance with Dragons* remained one book helps to explain the great tragedy of our time: the five-year wait between *Storm of Swords* and *Feast for Crows*, which was more than double the period in between all the previous installments. [It does not, of course, really do much to explain the even greater tragedy that was the six-year-wait that befell *Dance*.])

The final result was that *Game*, *Clash*, and *Storm* ended up constituting the first, expository act; *Feast* and *Dance*, the second, cliffhanging act; and *Winds* and *Time* – which would ultimately be renamed *A Dream of Spring* in the years that followed – being the third, climatic act. And just to ensure that readers playing along at home would still be able to make heads or tails of his new, more-than-doubled series, Martin inserted epilogues into those act-ending installments. (Well, all right, the fact that he had initially planned on ending each of his original three books with epilogues is probably the more important rationale behind that decision – but it's still advantageous for us home players. And there are a lot of us.)

His series – at least in theoretical form – was finally complete.

## Kings, Gaming and Clashing and Feasting

There are multiple story threads in George Martin's ever-more-sprawling tale (and that's even excluding the myriad Dunk and Egg novellas), and they sometimes do and sometimes don't intersect, at least in terms of plot, if not in theme. What has consistently remained in the foreground throughout all five published novels, and will more than likely remain entrenched in the spotlight for the final two, however, is the political dance that is ubiquitously called the game of thrones in the Seven Kingdoms of Westeros.

The particular step this dance takes on in act one is, of course, the War of the Five Kings. *A Game of Thrones* takes House Stark and moves them down south to the capital for the first time in their several-thousand-year history, allowing them to intermix – explosively, in the case of House Lannister – with the other leading families. The resulting animosity between the two great houses quickly bubbles over into the mobilization and engagement of armies, which quickly transforms the (more-or-less) peaceful surroundings into a scorched warzone and which results, by book's end, in there being three kings. *A Clash of Kings* is the climax of the war, with two more sovereigns throwing their crowns into the mix, one losing his bid for the Iron Throne along with his life, and another utterly routed on the battlefield, forced to retreat – permanently, thus far – from the center stage of the conflict. And *A Storm of Swords* is the denouement, showing how the vast majority of the monarchs, along with the war itself, are ended and a tentative, halting peace starts to settle over the land.

In this early, heightened phase of the narrative, jockeying for power typically manifests itself in the creation and maneuverings of armies. How can King Stannis Baratheon find enough men to invade King's Landing? Just how will Lord Hand Tywin Lannister finally crush that nuisance, Robb Stark, in the Riverlands? What is the perfect timing for King Balon Greyjoy to strike against the North? The underlying politicking that clogs noble life, of course, still hangs ominously in the background – as is evidenced by the Dark Lord of the Sith-esque machinations of Lord Varys and Petyr Baelish – and occasionally erupts dramatically into the foreground, particularly when Queen Cersei Lannister endlessly duels against her Imp brother, Tyrion, but the author's and the reader's attention both are squarely set on the bigger picture of the war.

All this changes with the act break. As the first act comes to a close, so does the War of the Five Kings, and so, too, have the lives of most of the predominant power players thus far all across Westeros: Tywin Lannister, Eddard Stark, Jon Arryn, Jeor Mormont, Oberyn Martell (to a lesser extent). The next generation finally is given the chance to step firmly and irrevocably into the ruling ring, and what once were whispers behind lordlings' backs now become royal decrees; the vast majority of act two is focused not on battles, overt or clandestine, but on the actual, tedious task of ruling, and just how Cersei is able to function as regent or Jaime Lannister as lord commander of the Kingsguard or Littlefinger as the (temporary?) Warden of the East (or Jon Snow as head of the Night's Watch or Euron Greyjoy as monarch of the Ironborn or Daenerys Targaryen as the [temporary?] ruler of Meereen – the list goes on and on).

But the game of thrones, of course, never ceases. Once a new class of lords has ascended to power, the next class shuffles in and starts the game anew; the Tyrells rush to fill the vacuum in King's Landing, just as Balon's younger family members do in the Iron Islands and Lord Wyman Manderly does in the North. *A Song of Ice and Fire* is not unlike *The Sopranos* in this way – the first season may have been devoted to Tony becoming mob boss, but all subsequent seasons were about his trying to secure the position against the ever-changing sea of newer and younger faces (life in the Mafia tends to end in death or incarceration – who knew?) in his Jersey family and against the increasingly belligerent actions of the New York family.  The tide, it seems, never recedes.

And, sure to form, the second act ends on the cliffhanger of having the current and still-brand-new regimes across the Seven Kingdoms hovering precariously on the precipice.  Cersei is on trial for her life, Jaime may very well be walking into an insurgent ambush, the Boltons (the new Wardens of the North) are embroiled in war, and Jon Snow has been stabbed, possibly to death.  (All of which is not to mention, of course, the arrival of a certain Aegon Targaryen and the first invasion of Westeros in three centuries.) That the scheming of and repositioning around thrones will continue in act three obviously goes without saying; what's left up in the air at this point is whether we see the cycle continue and have the newest generation of nobles – say, Mace Tyrell and his family – shuffle off of this mortal coil, as well, or if George will stick with his current crop of leaders and show how they manage to break the constant cycle of violence and conquest in Westeros, if only for a little while.

### Among Others

One of the truly remarkable elements of Martin's story is its insertion of the real danger to Westerosi society quietly in the background, unbeknownst to the feuding lordlings (and done in such a way as to be the almost perfect execution of Alfred Hitchcock's storytelling adage:  show the audience the bomb under the table so that the actions of the characters around the piece of furniture take on several new levels of tension, meaning, and depth).  The only irony here is that its effectiveness was, more than likely, much greater when his series was only three books instead of seven; readers tend to get mired in the minutiae of the surroundings and, at times, to not see the trees for the forest.

We are talking, of course, about the Others, and their presence in the narrative literally from the very first chapter sets the background action for the entirety of the series – but background action it simply is, despite the importance that their first appearance would otherwise have the reader believe.  In act one, the Others are, to invoke a modern metaphor, down the street; they're close enough to occasionally hear from your window, and the neighbors are certainly getting worked up, but they're still a good distance away.  The only exposure to them in *Game* is when the brothers of the Night's Watch range a decent distance from the Wall.  By the time we reach *Storm*, they're making good progress on their march southward, but, again, they're still only at the Fist of the First Men – and this, it seems, is just the very first wave of their host arriving.

The second act has the White Walkers starting to approach the end of our driveway, destined to gang up and prepare to traverse the very short distance that is the front yard.  Not only have they reached the somewhat remote location of Hardhome (infesting the woods and even the waters around the only true wildling village), they're also starting to pick off the runaway stragglers of Mance Rayder's failed assault against the Wall, meaning they're now well within striking distance.

The inevitable outcome of act three will be, of course, the Others pounding on the front door (or maybe, if they're smarter than the slow-moving wights would have us believe, on the side or even back entrance, as they just may be able to secure some passage *around* the Wall instead of trying to burst *through* it). Their appearances across the five novels are scattershot, at best, but the distances traveled in between them is undeniable, and, after all, as Anton Chekhov has famously decreed, if ice zombies appear in the background of act one, they *must* be utilized in all-out war in act three. The invasion, real or attempted, of Westeros is imminent. It is known.

(Are the Others one of the longest-running – and, therefore, just possibly one of the most tenuous – plotlines in *A Song of Ice and Fire*? Yes, absolutely, and the immense dangers of stringing a late-game development out so unfathomably long and across so many thousands of pages is one of Martin's biggest narrative gambles, Chekhov's gun or no. But, then again, the late-game [re]appearance of Aegon Targaryen is another – and far more subdued – story thread, having been planted all the way back at the end of *Clash*. This is to say: anything goes in Martin's convoluted literary landscape.)

But what is also known is, perhaps, the ultimate narrative purpose of the supernatural monsters (at least, thus far), and it is thematic rather than plot-based: only when juxtaposed against such a profound existential threat can the nobility's constant jousting against one another in their games of thrones be revealed for what it truly is – trivial, jejune, and, George seems to be whispering in our ear, pointless.

Maybe these strutting, swaggering lordlings *deserve* to be zombified.

*Meanwhile, across the Narrow Sea...*

The White Walkers may be the most buried of all the narrative strands, but it is Daenerys Targaryen's long and involved arc that is the most separated and, typically, the most isolated of all of the airborne balls in George Martin's mad juggling act. How appropriate, then, that hers may very well be the final, series-concluding thread.

In the first act, we see Dany quite simply come into her own. This is the most blatant in *Game of Thrones*, when she becomes a woman grown psychologically and emotionally and is rewarded for her rite of passage with the first dragons hatched in 150 years. There is the lateral drifting of *Clash of Kings*, which ends in the conscious and resolute decision to craft her own army and spin her own strategy of invasion – which naturally leads to her taking the full responsibility for her actions by making a home, no matter how temporary, of Meereen. She is finally a queen by the end of *Storm of Swords*, even if it's of the wrong kingdom on the wrong continent and among the wrong people.

Act two, as previously noted, is mostly predicated on the next phase of her coming of age, this time as a ruler. But the end of this particular narrative chapter is very intriguing: after many volumes of the Westerosi not knowing of the Mother of Dragons, word finally reaches the Seven Kingdoms, and several factions deploy in a frantic race to assimilate her, one way or another, into the political machinations of (or, in the case of the Citadel, around) the Iron Throne. The woman who has consciously decided to separate herself from her homeland is being resolutely drawn back in – if the power players have anything to say about it. And they almost always do.

The final act, then, will deal with Dany making landfall on Westeros, a not-insignificant feat that we've been waiting the past 16 years to see. It is currently believed that her presence will almost immediately upset the political status quo on the continent and completely reset the game of thrones, but it's not a given – particularly in a story that has been so prone to throwing us zigs instead of zags – that she'll quickly obtain her crown, if she does so at all. Perhaps she'll defer to another faction, such as the true (if, indeed, he *is* true) heir that is Aegon, or perish in battle against the Others.

But this is precisely what makes her particular conclusion so inherently exciting and so vastly influential: Daenerys is the full embodiment of both of the other throughlines. She will be the ultimate game changer in the political jostling of the lordlings as they flock around one throne or another, and she will be the ultimate weapon – both offensive and defensive – in the coming battle against the forces of ice and darkness. How exactly each of these three dominant storylines pay off, in what order, and in what precise relation to the others is, of course, the ultimate question we have, both as students of narrative theory and as readers of high-quality literature (let us just hope that it doesn't turn into another Meereenese knot, which would be exponentially more tragic than any previous obstacle or delay). It is enough for now simply knowing that we have so many ducks lined up neatly in a row, waiting to be knocked down by a precision marksman.

# THE TELLTALE KNIGHT

*The narrative parallels and foreshadowing of the
Tales of Dunk and Egg*

Mimi Hoshut

In late 1998, a few months prior to the UK publication of the hotly anticipated *A Clash of Kings*, an anthology titled *Legends: Short Novels by the Masters of Modern Fantasy* was published. Edited by science fiction author Robert Silverberg, *Legends* comprised 11 novellas penned by noteworthy fantasy authors, each story's setting unique to its respective author's fictional world. True to its titular promise, the anthology's authors were the biggest names in the SFF kingdom – and George R.R. Martin was certainly no exception.

Although *A Game of Thrones*, the first step into the massive *A Song of Ice and Fire* saga, had been published only two years prior, Martin was a well-established author even before the onset of his magnum opus. In 1976, he released a collection of novellas titled *A Song for Lya* that was honored by the '77 Locus Poll as the best short story collection of the year. By the late '90s, he was a bona fide genre darling, with a smattering of award-winning novels and short stories spanning 20 years of writing. In conjunction with a solid decade of penning teleplays and story editing for television, two conclusions were undeniable: (1) Martin was certainly a SFF legend, and (2) his short writing story skills were Not to Be Fucked With.

*The Hedge Knight*, Martin's contribution to *Legends*, stands testament to his strength as a novella writer. When frequently questioned by hordes of excitable fantasy fans on the elusive subject of How to Write Epic Fantasy, he consistently suggests that one begin with penning short stories. *Hedge Knight* and its sequels, *The Sworn Sword* and *The Mystery Knight*, are chief examples of short-form writing at its pinnacle. Although readers of the *Song of Ice and Fire* series associate Martin with the epic scope and size of its constituent novels, it can be argued that these novellas are primary showcases for his storytelling voice and perfect literary pacing.

The three stories, each published in different anthologies over the course of 12 years, fall under the umbrella referred to as the Tales of Dunk and Egg, and beyond their proficiency as excellent standalone examples of Martin's short story prowess, they are deeply relevant to the *Ice and Fire* novels. Although they are frequently recommended as separate, tangential pieces of canon, the significant contributions they provide to Westerosi lore and the many-layered connections they form to the series proper cannot be denied. In addition to extending and colluding with Martin's rich history of the Seven Kingdoms, the novellas serve to texturize the canvas of the world with an in-depth view of the political, social, and economic climate during a time period predating the opening of *A Game of Thrones* by 90 years. Furthermore, the connectivity of the novellas to the series provides a new perspective for events occurring or referenced in the novels. And, finally, on a speculative note, the distinct parallels drawn between characters in the two series could potentially represent more than a few nods at continuity; the commonalities are sometimes thought to hint at future plotlines and twists in the upcoming *Song of Ice and Fire* novels, which would be consistent with Martin's uncanny ability to foreshadow events well before they ever come to fruition.

The novellas read like a standard Martin POV chapter – written in third person, but so rife with conscious narrative and so emotionally charged that they may as well be firsthand perspectives. The reader is instantly transported to Ser Duncan the Tall's oversized, clumsily self-conscious shoes. Despite perpetuating a continuous thread that stresses Dunk's impressive height while underscoring a self-deprecating characterization of being slow-witted, Martin writes a character who betrays the formula for a simple-minded giant. Dunk's character mimics the reader's introduction to the canon of Westeros, a learning process that endears him as an accomplice to the experience. The events and pacing of the short stories stand apart from the norm established by the *Ice and Fire* novels. While the series is noted for its gray characters and apparent moral relativism, the Dunk and Egg stories stand apart by being underpinnings of a parable. Dunk's nobility of spirit represents the concept of a true knight, and he is lauded by the smallfolk as "a knight who remembered his vows." His lowly stature and humble beginnings free him of the vanity, entitlement, and self-serving grandeur that color the behaviors of the rich, noble, and properly knighted. The characterization establishes a framework for all three novellas: a hedge knight who stays true to vows he never actually took and who always chooses the chivalrous high ground in a world that is normally dominated by a pervasive moral ambiguity.

Aegon Targaryen, on the other hand, brings humor and verve to a story that could otherwise feel didactic in its plotline. In stark contrast to the knight he serves, Egg is quick-witted and brash, prone to occasional bouts of princely opinions and precocity. The relationship he forms with Dunk is integral to the growth of both characters. Despite the stark difference in their backgrounds, he becomes a little brother to the hedge knight and demonstrates the respect and camaraderie that can be achieved between a knight and his squire. Through their misadventures and close calls, Egg gains valuable insight into the everyday life and frequently-miserable plights of the smallfolk under his family's rule. Like Dunk's character, Egg's lessons mirror those of the reader's, ever enhancing the feeling of being complicit in the deepening understanding of the Seven Kingdoms and the reality of daily life in the realm.

The novellas serve to do far more than establish parables about chivalry and the meaning of knighthood, however. They introduce and build on the knowledge that a reader obtains from the novels alone, with a level of depth and scrutiny that serves as an important foundation for an understanding of Westeros history. Chief among the expository elements is a firsthand account of the Targaryen lineage. As *A Game of Thrones* opens, the line of dragonkings had been overthrown by Robert's Rebellion roughly 15 years prior. As a result, the reader's grasp of Targaryen history is presented through the filter of multiple POVs, slowly and sedately through the evolution of several more books. The rudimentary facts are presented:     Aegon the Conqueror invaded Westeros and subdued six of the seven kingdoms under his rule with the might of his three dragons. His bloodline continued to sit upon the Iron Throne he established over the course of nearly 300 years, until Robert Baratheon raised a rebellion and usurped the kingship for his own. The remaining Targaryen children were either murdered or exiled across the narrow sea, which leads to Daenerys Targaryen's ascent to reclaiming her birthright in the series proper. This much is familiar, from the context of the novels – a portrait of the last Mad King, the famous Targaryen trait of insanity or glory, the bloodline's obsessions with dragons and wildfire. Through nearly every character's POV, the fall of the Targaryens is remarked upon as a history lesson, an extinguished family tree well-removed from its former grandeur.

The Dunk and Egg tales, however, resurrect it. Taking place roughly 80 years prior to the downfall of House Targaryen, the climate of the Seven Kingdoms is very much ensconced in the height of the royal family's power. At the opening of *The Hedge Knight*, Daeron II, the 12th Targaryen king, is enthroned. Dunk cites the common belief that Daeron and his sons had left the line of dragonkings secure for all time, thanks to a proliferation of princes that left no foreseeable shortage of male heirs – one of many instances of ironic narrative present in the stories. (The truth is that even in Good King Daeron's time, the heirs are severely reduced by a series of tragic happenstances, some of which the reader gets to experience firsthand.)

But the Dunk and Egg novellas reveal the reign for what it is, viewpoints offered from both the lowly hedge knight and his hidden princeling's sometimes-conflicting opinions. *Hedge Knight* brings Dunk in direct contact with the most prolific members of the royal house – pitted against one prince and aided by another – so the reader is given the opportunity to judge the famous bloodline accordingly. And his interactions bring to mind Jaehaerys II's quote: "Madness and greatness were two sides of the same coin, and every time a new Targaryen was born, the gods would toss the coin in the air and the world would hold its breath to see how it would land." It is unsurprising, then, that the reader can easily identify which Targaryen princes held to either side of the coin. It is more interesting, still, to see flashes of Daenerys's and Viserys's natures in their predecessors. Certainly there are elements of Baelor Breakspear's humanity and concern for a lowly hedge knight that echoes Dany's regard for the less fortunate population of Slaver's Bay. But the haughty entitlement witnessed in Valarr and Aerion Targaryen exists in her demeanor as well, and more certainly in her hapless brother's. The stark parallel between Viserys and Aerion, especially, is a notable correlation that leads to horrific deaths across the narrow sea for both, wrought purely by hubris.

This firsthand perspective of the male Targaryens also serves to humanize their house; the personality traits and characteristics of individual Targaryens prove to be greater than just the sum of madness and greatness throughout one famous family tree. Although House Targaryen is remembered in current Westeros as a historical figurehead for fire, blood, insanity, and power, the Dunk and Egg novellas refine the broad brushstrokes of reputation and remind readers that the Targaryen men were real people with much more nuanced dispositions. The *Song of Ice and Fire* novels certainly don't commemorate Daeron, the sardonic Targaryen characterized in *The Hedge Knight* by his rampant alcoholism and self-professed cowardice. Nor did they reveal that Maester Aemon of the Night's Watch was reputedly sent to the Citadel for training because he proved to be an "unpromising" prince. Maekar, their father, was especially interesting in his characterization, for despite being described as sulky and less capable than his brother Baelor, his irritability is tempered by his better judgment in the agreement to foster Egg to Dunk as squire. After the events of Ashford Meadow, we see Maekar struggle internally with the weight of responsibility for Baelor's death. "Some men will say I meant to kill my brother," he says to Dunk. "The gods know it is a lie, but I will hear the whispers till the day I die." This moment of grief is heavier still with his very real assessment of the situation. Maekar knows – and the readers know – that history is written in shades of rumors and half-truths, and that a Targaryen's reputation can be a disconnected premise.

In addition to introducing readers to Targaryen nobility at the height of their power, the novellas also increasingly focus on the events of the Blackfyre Rebellion. 14 years prior to Dunk's beginnings as a hedge knight, the realm erupted in a war prompted by the rift between Aegon IV's heirs. Infamous for his lechery and indiscriminate taste in paramours, Aegon the Unworthy sent his kingdom into a tailspin by legitimizing his multitudes of bastards, both lowborn and noble, upon his deathbed. He was also responsible for bequeathing the Valyrian steel of House Targaryen, Blackfyre, to his bastard son Daemon instead of his immediate heir, Daeron. The fallout escalated to civil war, as Daemon Blackfyre cast aspersions upon his half-brother's claim to the throne. Half the realm declared for the rebellious Daemon (the black dragon), while the other half remained loyal to Daeron (the red).

The war culminated upon the Battle of the Redgrass Field, a legendary clash that led to Daemon's end and cemented the reputations of key loyalist fighters. Chief among them were Baelor Breakspear, Maekar, and Brynden Rivers, better known as Bloodraven.

The wounds and grief caused by the Blackfyre Rebellion ran deep in the realm, and throughout his travels, Dunk draws ever closer to the tension left behind. In *The Sworn Sword*, he enters into the service of Ser Eustace Osgrey, whom he believed to be a loyalist. Upon discovering that the man he served once fought for the black dragon, Dunk is shocked and considers breaking his commitment to the minor lordling. But as the stories develop and Dunk's understanding of the realm deepens, the moral ambiguity of the civil war becomes ever clearer. Dunk – and the readers, by association – realize that good men fought and died for both sides, and that history is always rewritten by the victor. Daemon Blackfyre's reasons for rebellion were no less noble or important than Robert Baratheon's, but he lost while Robert triumphed. With this distinction, Daemon became infamous as a usurper and harbinger of chaos across the kingdoms. By stark contrast, Robert was lauded for ending the tyrannical reign of Mad King Aerys and celebrated for his destruction of the Targaryen lineage. Reality, it seems, is significantly less black-and-white than the books will allow.

A key component of the focus on the Blackfyre Rebellion ties back to exposition regarding Lord Bloodraven's character. Famed for his dangerous omnipresence via a network of unpredictable spies and agents, Bloodraven's name becomes synonymous with a whispered curse among the smallfolk who question the reach of his powers as King's Hand, and the extent to which he controls the weak-willed Aerys I. Although his name is rarely invoked in the *Song of Ice and Fire* novels, his character proves just as relevant to the events of current Westeros as it did during his controversial reign. Readers of the novellas will have recognized him instantly in the second Bran chapter of *A Dance with Dragons*. Suspended as a withering body intertwined in a tree, alive 89 years past his reign, Bloodraven proves to be the last of the greenseers – Bran's mysterious three-eyed crow.

Although the direct exposition of Bloodraven in the short stories is minimal, Dunk speaks to him at the conclusion of *The Mystery Knight*. It is during this conversation that Bloodraven refers to the uncanny Targaryen trait of experiencing dreams that function as prophecies. "Daemon dreamed that a dragon would be born at Whitewalls, and it was. The fool just got the color wrong." This is interpreted as a commentary on Egg's growth as a Targaryen, and foreshadows his ascent to the Iron Throne – a feat previously thought impossible, as Egg was the fourth son of a fourth son, on the very bottom rung of succession. (For this reason, his reign in later life earned him the appellation of "Aegon the Unlikely."

Not only do the novellas lay an explicit historical backbone for the series, they also feature a prominent parallel that hints at a less obvious connection. Prior to the publication of *A Feast for Crows*, Martin confirmed that a descendent of Dunk's would appear in the fourth book. The most apparent culprit would be that of Brienne, the Maid of Tarth, reputed for her less-than-lovely physical characteristics. She stands out among smallfolk as "freakish big," especially for a woman. Similarly, Dunk dubs himself Ser Dunk the Tall for the same reason – at an inch shy of seven feet by his late teenage years, he towers well above the average man. Colluding with their large, ungainly size, Dunk and Brienne both share the same doubts and self-consciousness regarding their mental prowess. Dunk's mental monologues read closely to Brienne's POV chapters, redolent with the same internal criticisms and awkward self-doubt.

And if the close correlations of their behaviors suggest similar personalities, then their plot trajectories mirror one another even more closely. The three Dunk and Egg tales follow the hedge knight on a journey across the Seven Kingdoms, serving any lord whose cause he believes in, and observing the life of smallfolk along the way. From the start of Brienne's POVs in *Feast*, she embarks upon a seemingly hopeless quest to find the Stark sisters – a task entrusted to her by Jaime Lannister, whom she has formed begrudging respect for and attraction towards. Brienne's chapters bring the reader closest to the travels of a hedge knight that can be found in the series proper and are replete with the realities of commoners' plights.

It certainly helps the correlation that both would-be knights travel with an endearing squire in tow, although Podrick Payne, perhaps, has significantly less claim to royalty. Both of their squires were acquired by persistent following to forge a close and protective relationship. Dunk and Brienne also possess a very similar moral code, consummately choosing the chivalrous high ground in a manner consistent with a knight's vows. Oddly enough, neither character is an anointed knight. This can be inferred from the context clues of Dunk's sheepish reticence where his knighthood is concerned, as well as Brienne's hapless gender identity. In *A Feast for Crows*, she observes Pod and thinks, "I am not a knight, no matter how many times he calls me 'ser.'" It is likely that both characters, suffering from a feeling of awkward displacement in their societies, turns to the code of knighthood to carve out a space for themselves. Holding to that moral code, choosing to defend the weak and helpless, eschewing their own self-interests and vanity for a greater cause – these are behaviors that both Dunk and Brienne uphold soundly, sometimes to their detriment.

It is worth noting that their two characters provide a notable contrast in the landscape of knighthood that throws the disparity of a knight's actions from his vows into sharp relief. Though Dunk and Brienne are separated by roughly a hundred years, the general disappointment with the realm's anointed knights remains consistent. The *Song of Ice and Fire* novels prove time and time again (especially underscored by Sandor Clegane's loathing commentary) that knights are rarely as noble as their vows. It is interesting, then, to see that the situation was clearly the same even in Dunk's era. Among the milieu of self-serving men who are unwilling to defend the weak, Dunk and Brienne stand out with their clumsy strides to honor knightly vows. It's very likely that both characters exemplify the moral code associated with the class because they are unable to join it; as outsiders, they live up to the standards of what is expected of a knight, because they were never allotted the privilege of becoming one. Those who are actually anointed seem to take their knighthood for granted and are less inclined to take their vows seriously.

Another explicit connection between the two characters is made even more apparent in *Feast* with Brienne's shield. Provided to her by Jaime from the armory at the Red Keep, her shield originally carried the black bat of Lothston.

Similarly, Dunk's inherited shield previously displayed Ser Arlan's winged chalice. Both of them commissioned their shields to be repainted. Brienne, unable to bear the arms of Tarth without identifying herself to those who would want her dead, opts for a sigil she remembers from her father's armory. Readers of *The Hedge Knight* may recognize the description instantly, as Brienne recalls "how she'd run her fingertips across the cracked and fading paint, over the green leaves of the tree, and along the path of the falling star." Tarth, not being referenced in Westerosi history as a particularly old lineage, is presided by her father, Lord Selwyn, referred to as the Evenstar. His title could easily be a reference to the falling star of Dunk's own sigil. If Egg became crowned at the age of 33, that implies that Dunk became commander of his Kingsguard at age 40, leaving Ser Duncan plenty of time prior to have quietly fathered children. Given this connection, it is highly plausible that Brienne could be his great grandchild.

The connectivity between the two characters casts questions as to the direction of Brienne's plotline in the remaining novels. Could her future hold accomplishments that mirror Dunk's – chiefly, rising to become lord commander of the Kingsguard? It seems unlikely, given her standing and current plight, and it could also have been previously accomplished by her inclusion in Renly's makeshift Kingsguard. And then there's their squires. Although Egg and Pod bear no resemblance to one another in terms of personality, their relationships to their respective knights are quite similar. It could be argued that Podrick Payne could go forward in future events to play a much more important role than being just a young squire. Finally, there also exists a question of Brienne's eventual fate, given her predecessor's tragic end at Summerhall. Even after her narrow escape from a premature end in *A Feast for Crows*, would Brienne go on to meet the same devastating death as Dunk?

Although never explicitly described in any canonical text, many contextual clues have been scattered in the *Ice and Fire* novels regarding the elusive tragedy at Summerhall. Multiple characters have made references to the event, alluding to the destruction of the castle, its connection with dragons, and the melancholy effect it had on Rhaegar Targaryen. At the time of the Dunk and Egg novellas, Summerhall is a royal castle chiefly inhabited by Egg's father, Maekar. Positioned upon the Dornish marches and previously occupied as a summer residence by King Daeron II, it was passed to Maekar while his brother Baelor held Dragonstone. The castle was destroyed by a fire in 259 AL, resulting in the death of both Dunk and Egg. At this time, Egg was better known as King Aegon V, and Dunk had transformed into Ser Duncan the Tall, Lord Commander of Aegon's Kingsguard. Although details of the events are unknown, Alester Florent's comment in *A Storm of Swords* firmly suggests that the tragedy resulted from an erroneous attempt to hatch dragon eggs. He compares it to the mad wildfire swigging of Aerion Brightfire, as well as the nine mages who crossed the sea to hatch Aegon III's cache of eggs. "Did we learn nothing from Summerhall?" he asks Davos. "No good has ever come from these dreams of dragons." In the same book, Ser Barristan tells Dany about her brother Rhaegar's melancholy connection to the castle, explaining that "he was born in grief." Because Rhaegar was born on the day of the fire, it is commonly believed that his birth was intrinsic to the unknown tragedy.

Although the event is shrouded in mystery, certain conclusions can be drawn regarding those who were involved. Egg, as the reigning king, was roughly 60-years-old at the time, with Dunk at 66 or 67 years. Both were present and perished at Summerhall, along with Egg's heir, Prince Duncan the Small. It is possible that Prince Duncan's wife, Jenny of Oldstones, was also present. Her friend, the dwarf seer who makes an appearance in *A Storm of Swords* as the Ghost of High Heart, recalls that she "gorged on grief at Summerhall." This phrase, in conjunction with the old crone's tears upon hearing what she calls "my Jenny's song," suggests that she may have lost Jenny in the Summerhall tragedy. On another note, the Ghost is also revealed by Barristan Selmy to be the woods witch who predicted the lineage of the Prince That Was Promised, explaining Egg's decision to marry his grandchildren Aerys II and Rhaella to one another. Barristan mistakenly believes that the old crone also died at Summerhall, even though the reader knows that she is alive by 300 AL and roaming the Riverlands. This does suggest, however, that she may have also been present during the event but somehow survived the fire.

The events in the Dunk and Egg novellas, while many years removed from the tragedy of Summerhall, could shed some light on the mysterious event. In *The Hedge Knight* and *The Mystery Knight*, a common thread surfaces in the form of a Targaryen's "dragon dream." Daeron, Egg's brother, reveals that he dreamt of Dunk before the two of them ever met. "I dreamed of you and a dead dragon," he tells Dunk. "It had fallen on top of you, but you were alive and the dragon was dead." Daeron is concerned that the dragon could be himself, so he asks Dunk to make certain that it's his brother Aerion he kills.

However, as it transpires, the dragon clearly symbolizes Baelor Breakspear, who died in the defense of Dunk's cause during the Trial of Seven. Years later, during the events of *Mystery Knight*, Daemon Blackfyre tells Dunk that he dreamed of "this pale white castle, you, [and] a dragon bursting from an egg." Daemon misinterpreted the dragon to be a literal one, hatched from Butterwell's prized egg. However (and as previously discussed), the dragon in this premonition is symbolic of Egg coming into his own as a Targaryen prince and, ultimately, a king. With these two precedents in mind, it is not unlikely that the disastrous attempt to hatch a dragon egg at Summerhall could have been the product of a misread dream or prophecy. Like Daemon's misreading, the dragon in this hypothesized dream or prophecy could actually have symbolized a Targaryen – in this case, Rhaegar. This would explain Rhaegar's birth on the same day his predecessors are attempting to raise a dragon, as well as the melancholy connection he bears to Summerhall that continues to haunt him throughout his life.

By presenting these possible parallels, the novellas bring an extra dimension of understanding to the Seven Kingdoms. Although seemingly disconnected from the series proper as a separate strand of stories, Dunk and Egg's adventures are arguably as important to the history and context of Westeros as the current novels are. They certainly provide Martin a chance to showcase his superior short story writing skills. When a reader becomes distracted from the caliber of Martin's craft by the multitudes of intertwined POVs and barrages of plot twists over several long books, it is important to look to the novellas for examples of his storytelling at its best. With tight pacing and clever, well-defined story arcs, the Dunk and Egg stories are worth reading – and re-reading – for the level of writing alone. Factoring in their weight and contribution to a full understanding of Westeros, they establish themselves as invaluable companions to their partner novels – a must-read and, certainly, must-analyze for every *Song of Ice and Fire* fan.

# AFTERWORD

*Just Desserts*

Dear readers, eaters, friends, and fans,

Over the past year, I have dined with the brothers of the Night's Watch, snitched fruit tarts from the kitchen with Arya Stark, and indulged in a startling variety of meats, root vegetables, and ingredients so strange they would never have otherwise come into my kitchen. My everyday has been eaten up (small pun intended) by fictional foods, and what started as a fun blog project has evolved into a beautiful cookbook.

With the publication of the official *Game of Thrones* cookbook, fictional food has gained another solid foothold as an up-and-coming genre. Readers looking for new ways to connect with their favorite stories can now sit down to a table with the characters over a bowl of onion broth and a heel of black bread.

Let me begin at the beginning. One evening in March of 2011, I was sitting with friend and fellow *Song of Ice and Fire* fan Sariann when we realized we were very hungry. Being the types we are, we thought first of dessert (to this day, we have no memory of what we ate for dinner) and quickly decided that the only thing for us was a heaping plate of lemoncakes.

Now, if you must understand one thing about us, it's this: we are creative overachievers. Of course we could have simply made some boxed lemon cake mix, or found a decent recipe online, and been reasonably satisfied. Indeed, a reasonable person might have been.

But we are clearly not. We had to find a medieval recipe. And a modern one. And take photos and review them and start a blog to share our findings with other fans. Finding the perfect lemoncake recipes took months but was well worth it.

Thank goodness we didn't take the easy approach. My time as an innkeeper has been amazing, filled with so much good food and so much enthusiasm and support from other fans. Going from idea to blog to published book was every bit the fairy tale story that one won't find in *A Song of Ice and Fire*. And I think we can all agree that it's that harsh realism and level of detail that makes *Ice and Fire* such a compelling story.

My favorite detail, of course, is the food.

With the subtle artistry of his language, Martin makes our mouths water and coaxes us to yearn for lemoncakes just as much as Sansa does. As her circumstances change throughout the books, we too yearn for the simple sweetness of the early days at Winterfell before we learned just how deep and dark the political schemes of Westeros run.

When Davos finds himself in a prison on the Sisters, the good food served him instead of stingy prison fare gives him reason to hope. In the North, when Samwell Tarly wishes he could be eating a pork pie, our stomachs grumble along with his. We hunger for these fictional meals the same way we hunger for the next book in the series.

But food also plays a more sinister role throughout the books. Sometimes it's used as foreshadowing, and other times to actually deliver a character's doom. Take a look at the fare served up at the Red Wedding:  thin leek soup, stringy beef, pickled calves' brains, and mashed turnips, all followed by an ominous platter of juicy pink lamb.

Then there's Joffrey's wedding feast, with the staggering 77 courses, the most memorable of which is, of course, the pigeon pie.  But is the pie just a ruse?  Perhaps it was the wine, not the pie, that carried the poison, although I doubt that would have saved the cook from Cersei's wrath.

Remember the honey-spiced locusts that Strong Belwas so eagerly scoffs down?  They clinch things in Dany's mind about Hizdar's plots.  Lord Manderley's three giant pies?    The North *definitely* remembers.  Weasel Soup was such a notable plot point that everyone remembers it, even though no one ate it.

In short, while the weighty descriptions of food in *Ice and Fire* might seem superfluous to some, they are an integral and valuable part of the whole.  Like the seasoning on a piece of meat, these details are the spice to the main dish of the story.  They elevate it beyond the simple act of telling a story, enabling readers to step into that setting.  I love this immersive kind of fiction and know you do, too.

So the next time you're reading, consider pulling up a tankard of mulled wine or a skewer of roasted meat.  I promise you won't be sorry.

Happy Eating,

*Chelsea Monroe-Cassel*
*Co-author of InnattheCrossroads.com and*
A Feast of Ice and Fire

# APPENDICES

*A note from the editor*

Just a few months after starting my freelancing work for Tower of the Hand, I thought it would be intriguing to pick the minds behind two of the biggest powerhouses in the *Song of Ice and Fire* community: TOTH and A Podcast of Ice and Fire. The former I interviewed for Corona's Coming Attractions, primarily a film and television site (which I've been freelancing for since the end of 2010), since it would allow readers primarily familiar with the HBO series to get exposed to the wonderful resource site and the even more wonderful novels. The latter I did for TOTH directly, keeping the love within the *Ice and Fire* community.

Both were a great deal of fun to initially do and are collected here to provide background information on the personalities and institutions on display in this book. There is, of course, a not uncertain sense of irony embedded in these articles now, given how closely we two sites have since become (thanks, in no small part, to *A Flight of Sorrows*).

# APPENDIX I

*What's a Game of Thrones without the Tower of the Hand?*

Marc N. Kleinhenz

Original publication date: 07.03.11
Original venue: CoronaComingAttractions.com

The *Game of Thrones* might have just ended a few weeks ago, but the *Dance with Dragons* will be starting a few weeks hence.

There is much anticipation amongst the fandom community, as one can imagine after having been forced to wait six long and grueling years for this next installment, and Tower of the Hand, one of the premiere fan sites on the web, has been ramping up for the big event for the past month, including a countdown of the most-hated characters and a series of essays recapping where all the various story threads currently stand. (Afraid that pursuing such articles might ruin future books/television seasons for you? Don't worry – one of TOTH's most distinguishing factors is its scope filter, a magic wand that removes all references to future developments. Read easy, friends.)

But the heart of the site lies in its encyclopedia of chapter-by-chapter breakdowns of the books, character biographies, and in-depth essays on thematic developments and narrative interpretations.    That's *a lot* of material to produce, particularly given the intensity of author George R.R. Martin's ravenous fanbase, which led me to a very simple question:  just who the hell is responsible for creating and maintaining all this stuff, anyway?

Johnny Jasmin and Alex Smith, co-founders of Tower of the Hand, were nice enough to indulge my flights of fancy.  Below is our little nerd-tastic chat, which will help kill some time until *Dance with Dragons*'s release or *Game of Thrones*'s second-season premier.

**All right, first things first:  who's responsible for all this?**

John Jasmin, the Captain of Code and Bastard of the Blog:

My first attempt at an *Ice and Fire* site began in 2001.  I typed all the names from the first book's appendix into an Excel spreadsheet and tried to programmatically generate family trees from it.  It was more a proof of concept (and geeky challenge) than anything else, but it grew into my Blood of Ice and Fire site the following year.  Around 2004, I wanted to expand on this and offer something more polished.  Chris Holden had written a series of popular FAQ articles, and he agreed to collaborate on a new site.  We named it Tower of the Hand, though we didn't make much progress beyond that.

Alex Smith, Lord of the Chapters and Keeper of the Keys:

I first conceived of my site in fall 2003 because I loved the Encyclopedia WOT for Robert Jordan's *Wheel of Time* and was disappointed that nothing similar existed for *ASOIAF*. My site layout was pretty much an exact copy of theirs because I really have no web design skills, but I did contact Bob Klutz and Gary Kephart first to receive their blessing so they would not think I was just thoughtlessly ripping them off if they ever stumbled across my work. I began creating the site in October 2003 and posted it a year later once work on *A Game of Thrones* was finished. I kept adding to it over the next year until John contacted me about Tower of the Hand.

Johnny:

Yeah, it wasn't until mid-2005 when I discovered Alex's encyclopedia and asked him to join, too, that things really took off. By then, I had a design and a framework in place, but it was Alex's content that ultimately defined the site. We officially launched on November 8, 2005, the day *A Feast for Crows* was released in the US.

**With that said, walk us through the update process for each new novel. Do you make additions to the site or notations in the book as you read, or do you wait until you've completed it? And just who is responsible for writing the chapter summaries?**

Alex:

The chapter summaries as well as the reference pages for all the characters, houses, etc. are written by me. As I mentioned before, when the site launched, the first three books were already out, so *A Feast for Crows* is the only book that has been added since. For that book, I plowed through the text in two days, which gave me a general idea of how all the chapters and characters fit together, and then I did a close reading of each chapter, one at a time, doing the summary as I read, and then filling out the individual character and other reference pages for that chapter before moving on to the next one. Because all the important information for each chapter is written as I go, there is no need to annotate, because I can just refer to what already exists on the site to know where to go if I have to go back and check something. I like to update the site chapter by chapter as they are completed rather than wait until the end. In the case of *AFFC*, the entire process took a little over four months. While I hope to plow through this material a little faster, the timeframe may still be about the same since there are substantially more chapters.

**How many iterations does each chapter summation/character bio go through?**

Alex:

Each chapter summary was completed in one pass, but I have since been slowly (emphasis on *slowly*) going back through and revising them because since finishing *AFFC*, I have developed a new philosophy of including most information in the summary itself rather than putting historical and cultural information in notes at the end. Character bios iterate by chapter and expand as I complete each summary. In general, since I know what happens throughout the book, I try to anticipate the sentence/paragraph structure and do not have to rewrite too much earlier material as I move forward. Once again, these are in a state of flux right now as I move more information out of the notes into the main body of each summary and add more chapter references, as well.

**How important a part does feedback emails, such as corrections on facts or the small details, play?**

Alex:

User feedback is a great source of information for corrections and small details. While I catch a fair number of mistakes on my own, the sheer amount of text I have written while feeling pressure to post new material as quickly as I can has led to a great deal of typos, which our readers are often kind enough to point out through our internal message system. I fix those whenever I can. We also have a proofreader, Kohl Liang-Weissgerber, who has been going through my text over the last couple of years to fix what he sees, as well.

**You started the site with this particular section. But how long, exactly, did it take for everything to get up and running?**

Alex:

Yeah, when Tower of the Hand first appeared, this pretty much was the entire site. John and the essay writers he has established a relationship with have taken the site in many other fun directions with quizzes and analysis and frequent blog postings, but in the beginning, the site was basically a union between John's family tree work at Blood of Ice and Fire, my chapter and character summary work at An Encyclopedia of Ice and Fire, and Chris Holden's textual analysis at his Song of Ice and Fire FAQ. Like I said, I began work on my original site on October 6, 2003, and posted the first version of the Encyclopedia online a year later to the day after I had completed all the information for *A Game of Thrones*. I completed the second book in July 2005 and was still working on *A Storm of Swords* when John contacted me a month or two later to see if I was interested in merging our content to form Tower of the Hand. I then worked furiously to have the entire series finished by the time we opened our doors on November 8, 2005.

Johnny:

It amazes me how quickly that first official version of the site came together. By the time Alex came on board, the site's design and framework were in place. We targeted November for our launch, figuring three months to be enough time to get everything else up and ready. How naive. Alex spent the whole time editing and reformatting the chapter and character summaries, and I was redesigning and fixing bugs until the very last minute. We've since added several interactive features to the site, but the encyclopedia remains Tower of the Hand's biggest draw. Recently, we launched a mobile version of the site so readers can quickly access the encyclopedia from their phones, and we hope to release apps for the iPhone and Android, too.

**There are a number of background/preparatory essay writers who help contribute to the site. How did they come about signing up?**

Johnny:

I've always thought analytical essays would be a perfect addition to all the reference material we provided.     When Chris was unable to contribute more than his original set of FAQ articles, I managed to coerce some of our more brilliant commenters to post a topic every now and then, or to participate in a roundtable or two. Eventually, and to our great fortune, people started coming to us, asking if we could post an essay that they'd written.   Miles Schneiderman (ghostlovesinger) was the first, and he's since delivered a wonderful series of essays that follows up on our now-outdated FAQ.   Stefan Sasse similarly authored an exhaustive look at the major houses through the first four books, a perfect recap leading into *A Dance with Dragons*. We've been so lucky to feature all these talents on our site, and we look forward to hearing everyone's thoughts on the new book.

Alex:

Yeah, John signed up all the essay writers and the like. I am responsible for the artwork on the site. I was always a fan of Roman Papsuev (Amok)'s character portraits, and I noticed that several sites around the web displayed versions of them, so I wrote him an email and asked for permission to use them on Tower of the Hand, as well, which he was fine with. When it came to heraldry, I knew that Westeros.org did not give permission for people to use their extensive collection for the understandable reason that they worked closely with Martin himself to design heraldry for every last house in the series and want to protect the integrity of that body of work. I had actually first approached Stig Greve (Cadmus) to use his designs back when I was working on An Encyclopedia of Ice and Fire, where I used the shields of each POV character's house to add a little color to the chapter summary page.

He was even nice enough to create a Night's Watch shield for me for that purpose. After Tower of the Hand was up and running for a bit, I decided to contact him to see if we could use his heraldry on our house pages, as well, and he was happy to oblige.

Be sure to check out the fruits of Alex's labor over the course of the next few months, as *A Dance with Dragons*'s vast new material is poured over, analyzed, and added to the immense Tower of the Hand databank. Oh, and there's bound to be a few dozen new essays, too, including several by yours truly.

# APPENDIX II

*The Creaking Door of House Manwoody*

Marc N. Kleinhenz

Original publication date: 08.01.11
Original venue: ToweroftheHand.com

A Podcast of Ice and Fire, which first bowed in Mach 2008, brings several passionate hosts (whose number seems to fluctuate on a consistently semi-regular basis [not unlike the number of POV characters witnessed in the *Song of Ice and Fire* novels themselves]) and a wide array of guest hosts together to discuss the television series, reenact scenes from the books, and generally dish Westerosi gossip. It is certainly an entertaining production, littered with off-topic banter and choked full with inside jokes – so many, in fact, that an entire webpage has been devoted to tracking and explaining them – but it has also proven to be a somewhat controversial one, as well, making for the perfect set-up for a roundtable chat.

**It seems to me that your podcast has essentially gone the way of *A Song of Ice and Fire* – originally intended to head down one (rather serious or, even, academic) path, only to take a circuitous and oftentimes silly road. Just how divergent has everything been for you guys?**

**And how happy are you all with the way it's turned out?**

Amin:

Yes, you are right.   For the first few episodes, we just were feeling our way around, slowly getting to know each other.  We were, as far as I remember, planning to do an academic- or serious-style podcast.   Instead, we ended up becoming a very laid back and casual podcast, with tons of raunchy humor and inside jokes.  We weren't trying to be funny but ended up being quite humorous.   We have embraced lines from some of our worst-received podcast reviews, such as "a shocking lack of knowledge" or "a circle of spite."

Mimi:

Great question.
It has occurred to me frequently, recently (in light of all the podcast inside jokes being referenced by our listeners on the podcast forums), that we've arrived at a very different niche in *ASOIAF* fandom than originally anticipated.
When I first envisioned the podcast, in early 2008, I imagined a highly structured, organized show akin to Mugglecast that could produce consistent, professional episodes.  I also, at that time, had zero idea as how to go about recording, editing, and publishing such a concept.  In my original vision, each host on the show would have his/her particular segment and responsibility for episode material.
I did not expect our lack of experience and similar senses of humor to generate the result that it did, but it was inevitable.  Instead of structured

episodes with consistent segments, we essentially produce long, meandering conversations between friends. You don't talk to the same people regularly over the course of three years without developing camaraderie, and I think that underscores every episode we publish. Ultimately, as far as I'm concerned, that makes what we do so much more fun and has assured the show's longevity. The humor, disorganization, and general tongue-in-cheek attitude towards the material has also netted us somewhat of a cult following among *ASOIAF* fans. I'm very happy with that particular outcome.

Ashley:

I'm a stickler for details. I'm the guy that listens to podcasts and shouts at the screen when they get facts wrong and constantly grumbles about "If I had a podcast, I'd never screw up my facts... shame I have no social skills." So when Mimi came recruiting, I was like, "Oh, hell yeah! This'll either be awesome or really awkward." I, too, listened to the *Harry Potter* podcasts and thought we'd be similar to Pottercast, in that we were serious and proper, knowing I'm better at just spitting out facts than friendly banter, but my favorite *HP* podcast at the time was Allycast, a foul-mouthed, tell-it-like-it-is, raunchy, in-your-face podcast that quickly became one of the most popular *HP* podcasts out there. I couldn't be happier that we took the Allycast road; I'm not good at letting my sense of humor show, but through our constant teasing and banter, I've found it a lot easier to open up and just have a good time talking about a series I love. I think it's great that we're more like a group of friends, and that we have constant guest hosts, and that now our forums make our family even larger without it seeming like there's some sort of elitist circle between fans and producers.

**If this camaraderie, with both one another and the fandom community, has been your biggest joy, what has been the biggest disappointment?**

Mimi:

For me, there's two disappointments. Losing a host is always a letdown. Inevitably, old members of the podcast have dropped out due to time constraints and/or lack of interest in the material. It takes a lot of time and effort to keep this production up, so I understand when it's no longer feasible for someone to continue participating regularly, but it's still always a bit sad. Chris and Aaron were both hosts who signed on to the podcasting lineup from the very beginning, and listeners still reminisce about their episodes. Ashley 2 was fantastic, and I was definitely disappointed when she left the podcast.

The second is the negative feedback, of course. Everyone on the podcast knows I take criticism rather personally, since this show is my baby. It's a creepy, dysfunctional, and oftentimes perverted baby, but we do take a lot of pride in what we do. Again with the cult following thing – we're not an *ASOIAF* podcast for the average fan, especially not the serious/academic types that a fantasy epic of this magnitude tends to attract. I think a lot of these people listen to an episode expecting something more approachable, and they get turned off by the digressions, inside jokes, and stories about my father. Essentially, I understand exactly why our podcast is so divisive. But it's always disappointing when something that we put this much time, enthusiasm, and heart into gets dumped all over by people who are so intense in their dislike that I feel like I personally owed them a favor and failed. I know the internet breeds critics in everyone, but I still can't help being frustrated when people misunderstand our intentions.

Amin:

Mimi's answer pretty much covered it for me, particularly point two. I don't mind getting negative feedback, but I like it best when it is constructive criticism, not when there is intense negativity that is often inaccurate in itself. We've had plenty of both.

We can handle criticism. Apocalypse Dan (avernaith) was one of our first critics, actually. But he gave us constructive criticism, has guest hosted with us, and is now one of our biggest fans.

Ashley:

Mimi's answer is great. The criticism that bugs me is from the people who just don't get it, people who take us too seriously or don't realize that we're laughing at ourselves more often than not about our own ridiculousness. It bothers me when people make remarks about making their own podcast or getting other fansites to make their own for them to listen to, completely ignorant of the amount of time and work that goes into creating a consistent podcast.

**You've been "on the air" for three years already. Is there any plan for the podcast for the next three years, or do you guys simply wing it? Is there any endgame in mind?**

Mimi:

Amin pointed out recently that we have enough material to continue for three more years, if not even longer. Assuming that the show does not get cancelled, we will have episode discussions as well as our chapter re-reads (which, at this current speed, are going to go until we're all on Medicare).

Right now, there's no endgame in mind, and we haven't really discussed it. But if I had my way, we'd continue until the final book is released and discussed. I can definitely see the podcast slowing down between releases and going on more hiatuses over our lifespan, but I really enjoy the idea that we can be this go-to listening source for all existing readers, as well as new readers who will pick up these books years later.

Amin:

Yah, that's pretty much what I think on this question, too. =)

Ashley:

As long as there's constant new material – and with the TV show, that seems likely for a while – I don't think we'll have a problem continuing. I can see sort of slowing down our releases at times when there's little news to discuss, but I doubt we're going anywhere. The great thing about having a large crew and constant guest hosts is that even when we're low on numbers, there's a large pool of hosts to draw from, if need be.

# COLLECTOR'S EDITION

# FOREWORD

*Bendable Joints and Removable Body Parts*

*"I think we had best find you a new cloak," the king said, holding out his hand.*

I'm honored to be asked to write a foreword for this limited edition print copy of *A Flight of Sorrows*, the first book from the eminent website known as the Tower of the Hand. Now, the ebook already has a foreword, so one would think that writing a new one would be a little like stepping on someone's toes (in this case, Phil Bicking, who wrote the foreword, "And Now It Begins," for the ebook publication – so I suppose I really should call this foreword "No, Now It Ends," but it doesn't really feel like the whole spectacle surrounding George R.R. Martin's *A Song of Ice and Fire* is ending just yet, does it?).

The thing is, though, that some brand-new material has been written specifically for this edition, exploring the world of George Martin even further, and you better take notice so you're not thinking you're buying the same *Flight of Sorrows* all over again, and here I am, pointing out just that fact for you. Something about George R.R. Martin's saga has spawned a host of dedicated fans writing about Westeros; you hold in your hands one example of this (as for what that something is, well, that topic deserves a book all of its own). There is also the cookbook written by fans of the saga. I hear there's a book about Tyrion Lannister's dialogue coming out. Other essay collections are out there. Dozens of blogs dedicated to reading, re-reading, or discussing the books of Mr. Martin. Some fans even collaborate with Martin himself in order to publish material based on the novels. Even I, who hadn't really written anything before, had a book published (in which I gave *A Game of Thrones* and George himself the full treatment). Some might suspect that this rise of "fan books" means that people are trying to get rich on Martin's work. That's just crockety-crock, of course.

*A Song of Ice and Fire* is just that ridiculously compelling. Where once Tolkien fans wore buttons that said "Frodo Lives!" now Martin fans publish books in which they indulge themselves in the fantastic – and brutal – world of Westeros – and the fact that there is a market for books like this proves just how popular and captivating Martin's tale has become.

And so we have this new edition of *A Flight of Sorrows*, with new texts with new angles and new viewpoints. Here you will find a glowing appraisal of all things Dorne, a dynasty that came fairly late into the story – and yet House Martell, too, has grabbed the imagination of fans. Maybe you're more into the Targaryens, with their fascinating history. Or maybe you're like me, interested (some in my household would say "obsessed") in all things Westeros and just can't get enough of it (where is the Theon Greyjoy action figure with bendable joints and removable body parts?).

Martin's novels are so rich and complex that we've far from exhausted the material yet – and I haven't even mentioned the countless threads on various forums of ice and fire where everything is being dissected, analyzed, and speculated about. With that in mind, I can only hope we'll see a *Flight of Sorrows II*, and *III*, because these days, half the fun of being a fan is to read the opinions and thoughts of other fans and live the fantasy together (and, sorry, I can't help it – it's a great way to bide the time while waiting for the next installment in the saga).


*Remy Verhoeve*
*Author of* Waiting for Dragons
*and* Waiting for Winter

# INTRODUCTION

*The Princes Kept the View*

Marc N. Kleinhenz

What the hell were we thinking? (I can tell you right off the bat what we *weren't* thinking: that we'd ever be doing a physical copy follow-up, let alone anything with "collector's" or "edition" in the [sub] title.)

Throughout the course of 2012, we were thinking that, after seven years of doing the site and discussing largely the same chapters and debating exactly the same conspiracy theories in precisely identical ways, it would be exciting and just a little novel (no pun intended) to stretch out to new media and, quite possibly, in the process, push ourselves to new levels of analysis or discovery. We wanted to do something challenging, where we might just end up falling flat on our faces, and we wanted to do something where we would end up reaching out beyond the confines of our little corner of the internet to other individuals at other institutions that we collectively respected.

(Let's be honest: we were also thinking that, as a byproduct of our new endeavors, making just the tiniest bit of money – and please allow me to emphasize *tiny* – wouldn't be the worst thing in the world. We essayists at TOTH feel really, really bad that the two co-founders,

John Jasmin and Alexander Smith, pay for all the server fees and whatever other costs are associated with running a major website by themselves, out of their own pockets. And, for their parts, Johnny and Alex have repeatedly gone on the record that they feel really, strangely bad that they can't pay the rest of us for our efforts month in and month out. So I suppose this type of mutual guilt society was a formidable undercurrent of our interest at pushing the envelope.)

It turns out that the idea of doing a Tower of the Hand-related ebook was around a lot longer than I was, though it was never mentioned to me until nearly a year into my tenure at the site, after I had just released my own (literally last-minute and equally experimental) ebook, *It Is Known: An Analysis of Thrones, Vol. I.* The occasion of my being brought into the machinations of the editorial cabal was a seemingly-benign email between me and Johnny, discussing various bits of business about the site and the burgeoning marketing efforts for *It Is Known.* The date was Monday, April 2, 2012, a day which shall now live in infamy.

After going over a few different points, Johnny slipped this in at the very end of the email:

> *One other question I've been meaning to ask you. How difficult was it to get your book on Amazon? Alex, Kohl* [Liang-Weissgerber, the copy editor], *and I have been working for months on finishing an ebook version of our chapter guides (one of the more popular requests among our readers). I never considered distributing it on Amazon or such, but I am curious if*

*that would be a possibility for us. Any
insights here would be great.*

I'm not sure about insights, but I did have
lots of points of pontification. I called him up,
and we spoke about the various ins and outs of
self-publishing on the Kindle platform. I also
asked about the legalities of selling summaries of
someone else's original work, which I wasn't quite
sure of (nor am I now, to be perfectly honest),
and Johnny admitted he had to look further into
it.

And that was that for the next two or three
months.

The conversation, however, left a trace
desire nagging at the back of my mind to move
into the *Song of Ice and Fire* sphere, since, at the
time, it was still a pretty unexplored playing field
(I wasn't yet aware of *Game of Thrones and
Philosophy*, which had just released that March,
and the wonderful *A Feast of Ice and Fire* didn't
ship until May), and, furthermore, it was
something I knew we could nail in terms of
content, if not necessarily in terms of technique.
I brought the topic back up to Johnny on Friday,
June 29, but with a little twist.

*I was thinking… if you still wanted to go
ahead and publish all your summaries, you
should definitely include the solar
discussions, too - even if it's a separate
ebook.*

(Just for reference: the Solars of the
Tower of the Hand were intra-site roundtable
discussions that we had initiated just that year.
They were a great deal of fun, especially when
our readers got to join in with us, but work on *A
Flight of Sorrows* put them to a screeching halt,

and we have yet to get back on the roundtable bandwagon. It's something to consider for the Grand Redesign of 2014, I suppose.)

Immediately after firing off that email, however, a different idea had taken hold, exploding into something far bigger and much greater. Not even an hour-and-a-half later, I messaged Mr. Jasmin again, suggesting that we speak on the phone, since my exuberance precluded my sitting down long enough to compose another, elaborately long email.

Johnny being Johnny (read:   incredibly busy), he didn't respond to my enthusiastic missive, and so I had a long night of fitful sleep that night, my mind working the entire time, turning it over and refining it and coming out with an entire game plan.

The next day, Saturday, June 30, 2012, I spewed this out on my keyboard and very anxiously sent it over:

> *All right. I've thought about this the whole night – even in my sleep! – and I not only think it's a fully formed idea, I also just can't keep it to myself any longer.  =)*
>
> *This is the idea: we take you, me, and three other editors/essayists from TOTH (I'm thinking Alex, Stefan [Sasse], and Miles [Schneiderman], if they're game), and we write a series of essays to include exclusively in an ebook. We'll have two parts: one specifically for* A Song of Ice and Fire *and one about HBO's* Game of Thrones.
>
> *We'll each write a minimum of 3,000 words, although something closer to 4,000 would be ideal. This can be one 3,000-*

word essay, two 1,500, three 1,000 –
whatever we want to do. I'll be the
editor, handling the introduction,
uploading the book to Amazon, and
distributing the royalties. I'll also work on
getting someone really special for both a
foreword and an afterword (I'm already
thinking Ted Nasmith, if he has the time
[which is a really big if].)

Here's the cool part: we'll have five
additional slots left open for outside
authors. I'm pretty damn sure Elio
[Garcia, from Westeros.org] will want in,
as will, probably, Mo Ryan from The
Huffington Post. Other candidates I have
in mind are Amin [Javadi], James
[Poniewozik] from Time, David [Barr
Kirtley] from Wired, and/or Doug Cohen.
This will give us a grand total of anywhere
from 30,000 words (a really solid novella)
to 40,000 words (a short-ish novel).

What will the essays be about? I'm
thinking very specific, in-depth,
exhaustively-researched and -explored
material – y'know, like we already feature
on TOTH. But the catch is it has to be
exclusive and just different enough to
justify the purchase price to all our
readers, both present and future. So I'm
thinking we'll have at least one piece
feature the characterizations of ASOIAF,
one about the thematic motifs, another
dissecting (and predicting?) the prophecies
and more esoteric material, etc. It can be
a really good read, methinks... better than
Beyond the Wall. =)

*As far as a timetable goes, I'm thinking –
for right now, at least – rough drafts due
by August 1st, finals by August 15th, and a
publication date of late September/early
October. This will give us a nice little
bump at launch, another one (hopefully!)
at Christmas, and a final one during the
premiere/finale of season three. And
then, once we hit the one-year mark, we'll
drop the price by a dollar.*

*The first step in all this, of course, is
getting your permission/blessing/
participation. Once I have that, I'd like to
unroll it to the others at TOTH, and then,
from there, all the outside authors.*

*So... what say you? :D*

That I had forgotten about the existence of
*Beyond the Wall: Exploring George R.R. Martin's
A Song of Ice and Fire* is not at all an
exaggeration, even though it had been published
just ten days before, and it is, I think, a very
telling incident; as noted in the introduction to
the regular edition of *A Flight of Sorrows*, I had
been burnt before by various literary or
philosophic anthologies, some of which I was
forced to endure in my various undergrad classes,
and so I approached this latest one
enthusiastically-but-cautiously.        Furthermore,
much like Nintendo with both Sony and Microsoft,
I didn't consider the book to be a rival with, or
any other type of impediment to, my proposed
undertaking, and it slipped my mind entirely once
the writing and editing process started. I think
both time and sales have since borne this initial
hunch out.

(I should probably note, a year-and-a-half later, that I do, indeed, own a copy of *Beyond the Wall*, that I have enjoyed reading it immensely, and that I certainly look forward to seeing a second installment by James Lowder and guests. Please don't mistake my critical response to its announcement with animosity to its contents, analytical critiques not withstanding.)

Looking back, it's amazing how little our game plan actually changed from that initial idea to the book's publication on October 11, despite it being less than six months. And what did change – well, we'll get to that in a moment.

Just a few hours after receiving my novella of an email, Johnny responded.

*At first glance, this looks good to me. I received a review copy of* Beyond the Wall *a few months ago, but I haven't bothered to review it (yet) because I haven't been drawn to the topics. There's some good writing in there, but it's all critical and thematic analysis. If we assemble our own collection of writings, I suggest a different tack: speculative essays. Of course, we should call it something more academic (e.g.,* On text and subtext*), but it's more about letting our essayists do what they do best: debate and debunk crazy theories. These are usually the most popular articles on TOTH, so it stands that they'd be the most attractive to general readers, too.*

*If we do this, we should definitely include an essay on R+L=J, which is still the biggest mystery that most readers miss. From the TV angle, we can have someone analyze the necessity and/or effectiveness of, say, making Renly and Loras's relationship obvious.    Just spitballing ideas.  I'll pass this along to Alex, Stefan, and Miles, who I'm sure will be happy to contribute.  We've already spent the last week debating new essay ideas, so this is really only taking that one step further. 3,000-4,000 words should be no problem for those wordsmiths.*

*By the way, the summaries book has stalled a bit, primarily because some of the legal advice I've gotten seemed skeptical about its copyright and exclusivity (the latter an issue you recently reported with* It Is Known). *Writing completely original material sounds like a far more viable strategy.*

*Thanks for sharing this idea.    I'm very excited by the prospect of it.*

(The "exclusivity problem" I encountered with Amazon was simply the site sending me an email out of the blue asking if I did, indeed, own the rights to all the articles that were being collected and published as *It Is Known, Vol I.* Once they were given links to all the articles in their original form, they never spoke to me about it again – which actually ended up being a problem, as I had tried to follow-up with them several times about the whole incident.   The moral of the [side] story is that Amazon will pretty much bend over backwards for you if you're a customer, but if you're a self-published author on its platform, it'll regard you as little more than gum on the bottom of its shoe.  Contrasted with the way, say, Kobo deals with its clients, no matter how big or how small, it's a literal world of difference.)

My reply likewise took just a couple of hours.

> *I think doing one concerning Jon's parentage is a very good idea - maybe even condensing several unsolved riddles altogether into one piece, to make it somewhat unique/exclusive.*

> *I'm going to do one about the narrative structure of the books - about how the first three books comprise act one, etc. - since that was something that people really seemed to respond to in my "review" of ADWD. I think doing one about the two power players of the books - Varys and Littlefinger - would be fantastic, as well; they're the two who control all that we see and experience, and yet so few characters realize it. (It's also particularly interesting how they seem to be polar opposites in that we know what Varys wants but have no idea behind his motivations; for Baelish, we know what moves him, but we have no idea what form his endgame will be.)*

> *What I don't want is the decidedly scholarly feel of Beyond the Wall. While I'm normally all for this type of thing - my degree's in English, after all - it just fails to strike any type of resonance with me. Who cares about the evolution of the literary community's response to fantasy over the past 30 years? Why talk about what type of awards A Game of Thrones*

*received in 1996? I think the reviews on
Amazon tend to back this up.*

*By the by – Amazon is over its copyright
infringement witch hunt, so all is well
with the world.  For now.*

*I'm going to extend the offer to our group
of outside authors.  I'll let you know what
they have to say.*

What they had to say was that there was a
lack of time or money in the project, and most
were, therefore, not interested, at least on this
pass.  (To be fair, this *was* at the last minute,
particularly as far as these types of things go.)
Ultimately, after some back-and-forth, the only
ones who had big enough openings in their
schedules – or who weren't so concerned about
not getting paid a fee upfront – were Amin and
Douglas Cohen, who both told me in very short
order that they were in.

As expected, the other three TOTHers
were most definitely on board, which meant that
the first hurdle was cleared and that the second,
far scarier one was quickly approaching:   just
what the hell *do* we write about?

Three days later, on Tuesday, July 3,
Johnny included me mid-conversation with all the
others, debating whether an overarching theme
should be imposed on *Tower of the Hand: The
Book* or not:

*Adding in Alex and Marc, since the topics
are of interest to all of us right now.*

*Here's my weak suggestion for a theme:
mystery.  We could do a generic overview
of unanswered mysteries in the story, and*

*then more speculative essays on specific theories (e.g., a new R+L=J article). If anyone's feeling particularly literary, we could analyze GRRM's inclusion of a murder mystery (i.e., Jon Arryn) in a work that is better known for its fantasy/horror aspects, or we could break down the books' subtle uses of text and subtext.*

*I think Marc's essay idea on narrative structure fits in fine here, as do Stefan's existing "Southron Ambitions" essay and Miles's new prophecy analysis, though the latter would need to be reworked to serve as a standalone article.*

*Of course, I'm not saying we should limit the essays to a single theme, or that our writings should belabor the point. But I think the book needs to have some kind of connection, instead of being a collection of loosely-related articles. Beyond the Wall suffered from a lack of cohesion (and, bizarrely, redundancy, when two separate articles attempted to make similar points).*

My response followed on the same day:

*I'd also like to try and keep the essays between the novels and the series equivalent, if we can. Doug's and mine are about the former; how many do we have for the later? (Mo Ryan's will fit this category, if she fully commits to the project.)*

*Oh! I forgot to add something: the more I think about the various scopes of our various essays, and the various demographics that will potentially be picking this up (I suspect a number will be Game of Thrones-only enthusiasts), I think we'll absolutely have to lift the "scope" function of TOTH and apply it to each individual article.*

*It's a good thing we're TOTH: The Book, eh? >.<*

On Thursday, July 5, Miles chimed in.

*I can see the "mystery" theme working out. An attempt to prise out the series's secrets in a forensic-literature-analysis kind of way. I would be interested in that.*

*Here's the problem with the prophecy essay. It can't stand alone. At this point in the series, a full-blown analysis of the prophecy would need to reference R+L=J, the return of Aegon, and the death of Jon Snow, at the very least. I made reference to all those things in the new essay, but that, of course, was written with the ToTH audience in mind, assuming that most of them know about R+L=J and are aware of the earlier prophecy stuff, and if they aren't, encouraging them to look it up on the site. I also planned to write separate essays on the Jon and Aegon topics, which is why I briefly brought those up in the prophecy piece.*

*I just think that if we're going to include the prophecy in this book, we should include its companion topics, too. That's why I suggested the complete version for the book, since Johnny is writing about R+L=J. So far, it doesn't seem like anyone else is interested in tackling Jon and Aegon, though. If I'm the only one interested in writing about them, that's fine, but I certainly can't do it in 4,000 words. In that case, I would suggest that we relegate that entire series (prophecy, Jon, Aegon) to the site, for the time being at least, and I can write something different that would stand on its own and better fit the book's format. I am by no means bereft of ideas.*

*Marc, I think the scope thing is perfectly appropriate, given who we are, as you mentioned. As far as the novels vs. the show, I am personally kind of show-ed out, having written the episodic reviews this season. I'm enjoying writing about the books again.*

And, finally, Stefan followed up the next day:

*Of course, we could do a book about prophecies. I mean, the topic was tackled by Elio and Linda in their podcasts, Sean [Collins, from All Leather Must Be Boiled] and I did one about it with Steven Attewell [from Race for the Iron Throne], and there are articles about it out there. We could aim to create the definitive companion book about prophecies, which would differentiate the book from "just another essay" book.*

*I still think, however, that we could easily do several. eBooks aren't limited to*

*printing costs, and they are produced
rather fast. If we get some success with
them, we can easily expand or plan a
series from the start (and scrap it if
nobody wants it).*

And that, of course, is exactly what we
ended up doing: *A Hymn for Spring* ships on June
19, 2014, and if it's successful, we're already
eyeing an October 2016 release window for a third
book. Not that we're prone to getting ahead of
ourselves, though.

All the other ideas discussed in our back-
and-forth, however, ended up not panning out,
due to several reasons that were, not unlike the
byzantine *Song of Ice and Fire*, occurring
simultaneously and interdependently. With most
of the "outside voices" having passed, we opted
to ask A Podcast of Ice and Fire's Mimi Hoshut to
join our electronic ranks, despite her being a
somewhat off-the-wall candidate, given her lack
of analytical writing (though certainly not creative
writing, of which she routinely engages in). Her
addition crystallized for us something that was
hitherto lurking just beneath the surface: being a
"fan" publication, which we then began to
consciously center all our activities and design
decisions around. It not only made the ebook a
more fun and engaging project for us to work on,
it also further differentiated it from the likes of
*Game of Thrones and Philosophy* and *Beyond the
Wall*. (It also suggested the best personalities to
select for the foreword and afterword – and with
the addition of Winter Is Coming and Inn at the
Crossroads, *A Flight of Sorrows* succeeded in its
newfound mission of uniting as much of the fan
community under one roof as possible.)

With this new, pan-fandom identity, we
felt the need to include a minimum of 10 authors

lessen, settling instead on eight – which might have hurt the book in terms of length but made up for it by helping to make its contents, as well as its voice, more consistent and, dare I say, more unique. Additionally, the perceived requirements of an overarching theme likewise dissipated, a development which was helped along by the sheer logistical complexities of coordinating authors who lived at great distances from one another, particularly in such a remarkably short amount of time.

And this, in turn, caused a domino effect to ripple from the center out. No longer obligated to adhere to a specific subject, Johnny felt free to drop his "who are Jon Snow's parents?" essay, which, in turn, allowed Miles to switch from his prophecy summary to a topic that was nearer and dearer to his heart: whether dear ol' Jon was still alive or not. (Ironically enough, Stefan ultimately picked the prophecy torch up, though all of us were surprised at just where he ended up taking it.) And since Mo Ryan had to back out due to a plethora of writing obligations and a lack of time, the last person who was seriously interested in exploring the television side of things was gone, permanently removing that particular subject from *Sorrows*'s roster.

The result is a book that is, on the surface, substantially different from that initial flash of inspiration but that is also, in its form and effect, exactly the same. It's a book that catered to no preconceived notion, answered to no traditional publisher, listened to no voice of pragmatism or naysaying or condescension. It's kinda like *A Game of Thrones*, in its own way, and we're tremendously proud of it.

We're even more excited, though, to take all that we've learned and apply it to *Tower of the Hand: A Hymn for Spring* next summer... along with, possibly, a few of those abandoned premises.

# SAVORING THE TASTE?

*On the role of revenge in songs of ice and fire*

Stefan Sasse

The nobles of Westeros are committed to several principles, honor chiefly among them. But what do you do when your honor is stained? Do you appeal to the court, as any law-abiding citizen would, hoping to get justice in the bargain? Perhaps a hefty fine for the perpetrator, to make sure he doesn't do it again?

Yeah, I can't see it happening, either.

There are two reasons for this. First, there are no courts you could appeal to in Westeros – only liege lords and kings whose justice is arbitrary, at best. Second, the other lords expect you to wipe out the smear on your honor yourself. Perhaps because of this, many of the characters we meet in *A Song of Ice and Fire* are motivated, at least partially, by the desire for revenge. The Starks want to avenge the murder of Eddard. The Targaryens want to take revenge for the rebellion and the throne stolen from them. The Martells want to take revenge for the death of Elia and her children. Robert Baratheon started his rebellion out of a desire for revenge against Rhaegar Targaryen, and Brandon Stark dies for it, strangled in the Red Keep. Balon Greyjoy wants to take revenge on the Starks for being responsible for his downfall in his prior uprising. Brienne of Tarth wants to take revenge on Stannis Baratheon for the murder of Renly Baratheon. Walder Frey wants to take revenge on the Starks for betraying their oath. Catelyn Stark wants to take revenge on the Freys for the Red Wedding. The brotherhood without banners takes revenge on soldiers for committing war crimes. Chett wants to take revenge on Sam Tarly and Jon Snow for taking his comfy post away. Orell wants to take revenge on Jon for killing him. Wyman Manderly takes revenge for the murder of his son; Rickard Karstark takes revenge for the murder of his. Robb Stark avenges the murdered Lannister squires by killing Karstark. Littlefinger wants to take revenge on the whole aristocratic class that always looked down on him. And Arya Stark is citing the names of those she wants to take revenge on in her sleep, lest she forget.

These are just the examples that immediately jump to mind. I could continue the list, but I think you get the point: there are *a lot* of people set on revenge in the series. And only in rare cases does the revenge succeed in a way that gives the person taking it any joy in the long term. In the following, I will examine some examples in more depth because I will draw some conclusions on how revenge is placed within Westerosi society and what implications this has, as well as to the narrative function of revenge – and revenge failing to bring any success.

Let us start with the region most notorious for a vengeful desire: Dorne. The Dornish cultivated blood feuds even before Nymeria landed her ships, and the merging with the Rhoynar did nothing to quell their taste for revenge; feuds are remembered, almost revered, along generational lines. Just to give some scope: the Daynes of Starfall and the Oakhearts of Old Oak still remember battles and skirmishes from centuries past, and between Yronwood and Martell, enmities from the time of the war of Nymeria are still prevalent.

But all these past rivalries pale in comparison to the new blood feud with the Lannisters. Ultimately, of course, Robert was responsible, but the Martells have a pretty personal view on the people they want to see bleed: Tywin Lannister, for ordering the attack, and Gregor Clegane and Amory Lorch, for the murders. It is clear they are committed to revenge – after all, they want to continue the war after the sack of King's Landing and are only talked out of it by Jon Arryn – and never leave Dorne for the following 15 years. While the Dornish in general, being more of an ethnic people than the rest of the Westerosi, take this pretty personally, Prince Doran is the master schemer behind arguably the most complicated revenge plot that anybody in *A Song of Ice and Fire* ever envisioned (if you discount the Others, who have probably schemed their return since the Long Night). For Doran, revenge must be taken on the perpetrators themselves and everyone else responsible, in that order. The Prince of Dorne is nothing if not patient and methodical, so he divides his scheme into stages.

Stage one is getting at the murderers themselves, Gregor and Amory. (This is the only stage, by the way, which is pursued openly.) It's an open secret that they are the ones who did the killings, one only denied when asked directly, so the intent to somehow get at these is understandable. It's also the most realistic goal, because it's not really believable that Tywin would risk war just to save the likes of Lorch and Clegane. Of course, Doran can't really act on the issue; Gregor and Amory aren't stupid enough to go to Dorne, and he can't assault them openly (unless the Red Viper devises a plan for that, but that's another story entirely).

Stage two, therefore, is the attack on the person who most likely ordered the killings: Lord Tywin. It's not likely that any Dornish will get close to him.

Stage three consists of revenge on King Robert, who didn't give Elia justice and profited from the murders. This also means bringing down the realm in favor of the Targaryen heirs.

These stages take place simultaneously. Stage three is the one that begins right after Willem Darry's flight from Dragonstone, when the marriage pacts between Viserys and Arianne and between Daenerys and Quentyn are forged. But Doran wants successful revenge, and he knows he has no chance under the circumstances before the beginning of *A Game of Thrones*, so he waits. The War of the Five Kings, however, changes things drastically. The need for Dornish help not only gives him leverage to fulfill stage one (Tywin is totally prepared to give both of the murderers up), but it also places Oberyn in the perfect position for stage two. Never before has any Martell come this close to the Lord of Casterly Rock, and now Oberyn sits right beside him, judging his son and heir. This must be so sweet. And if you believe a common and plausible theory, Oberyn also finished stage two – Tywin might well have been poisoned already when Tyrion shot a bolt in his guts.

Until now, every part of this plan was deliberate, patient plotting and scheming and even (perhaps) assassinating. If everything had gone according to plan, Doran Martell's revenge would have been fulfilled: Robert, Tywin, Eddard, Gregor, and Amory are all dead. But here the truly terrifying part starts – neither Doran nor Oberyn (nor Arianne) is content with this success.

It's not that they want to cry out triumphantly; they want to see the world burn. The Martells take revenge farther than personal guilt or involvement into what happened. They want to see every Lannister dead. They want the Baratheon reign in pieces. And they don't care how many thousands must die for this.

Despite their revenge being practically completed, they're going through with their plan to facilitate a Targaryen return to the throne, not because they want to gain something (not once does Doran discuss the benefits for the station of House Martell after a successful Targaryen invasion), but because they want to cause as much destruction as possible. This ultimate motive is hidden very well behind the cold pragmatism of the game of thrones being played, but in his heart, the Prince of Dorne is just as irrational as his hot-blooded brother, Oberyn. It is hard to imagine the Martells stopping their revenge at some point, especially if the Targaryen heirs embark on a revenge trip of their own.

The same deadly spiral can be found in Arya. She also has very personal motives to hate people. In the beginning, she doesn't even really know if she wants the people on her kill list dead (she's a child, after all), and what that even means; instead, she's out for the usual twisted version of justice most revenge seekers claim to follow. But as her journey progresses, she not only expands her list constantly, she also starts a terrifying trend to take revenge on behalf of other people. Her first real act of revenge is the ordered killing of Weese, but before that, she kills Chiswick for boasting about the rape of the innkeep's daughter. Later, she finally has the chance to kill the Tickler, which she does. It's arguably an act of self-defense, but her stabbing him over and over and over again clearly indicates the cathartic nature of the killing. In Braavos, she again takes revenge on someone else's behalf, killing Daeron as to avenge his breaking of the Night's Watch oath. She also constantly tries to find the same kind of motivation in the Kindly Man, not believing despite all the rebuffs that someone could not share her desire to make the world right by murdering. It's a dark road she's walking.

Then there's Catelyn, who transforms into Lady Stoneheart. If there was any trait that really set Catelyn apart from most of Westeros, it was her strong emotional anchor, the source of her greatest strengths and weaknesses alike – arguably the thing that made her what she was. When she starts taking revenge on "the Freys," nothing of that anchor remains. Lady Stoneheart has nothing to live for. It is not possible to envision her at some point lying down, resting, and telling herself, "I'm done." She will continue killing people until she is destroyed. For now, she's murdering Freys as often as she can, whether or not they really had a role in the Red Wedding; it's not like she's seeking any evidence or corroboration.

But her thirst for revenge isn't limited to the people directly responsible for the Red Wedding, as evidenced in her killing of everything considered Lannister, too. Just look at Brienne and her travelling companions. Brienne rescued the children and killed Rorge, Ser Hugh was sworn to Randyll Tarly from the Reach, and Podrick is just a squire, but they're hanged for the offense of simply being around. The only one of the three Catelyn had any business hanging was Brienne, for breaking an oath to a dead woman that couldn't possibly be fulfilled, but things like that don't matter anymore because they're rational, and the thirst for revenge that drives Lady Stoneheart is as irrational as the one that drives the Martells or Arya.

Wyman Manderly also wants to kill every living Frey he can get his hands on. It's hard to say whether he has the same beef with the Boltons, although there doesn't seem to be a reason to stop at any point. Wyman also isn't shy of committing atrocities to fuel his thirst for revenge, like cooking people into pies and eating them. Would he stop when every Frey and Bolton is dead, or would he find new targets in the Lannisters who supported the Red Wedding? I seriously believe it's the latter, potentially making Manderly's quest an endless one, as well.

And, please, don't be deceived by the theoretically finite end of these revenge quests. Of course, at some point, everyone with the surname of Frey, Bolton, and Lannister could be killed, although it's possible that they will resort to killing bastards and offshoot family trees, too. But it's not a realistic goal, and it involves bloodshed on the scale of all-out continental war. That's the truly frightening thing about these schemes. The Martells are ready to bathe the south in blood, and the Manderlys drain the North even further than it already has been.

The only ones in this revenge-seeking league who have an actual goal beyond the blind quest are the Targaryens – even Viserys. They want the throne that was stolen from them (as they perceive it, at least) back and, of course, to punish the perpetrators. But you can instantly see the difference when they talk about their plans: Viserys and Dany have a very, very limited kill list (Viserys talks of Tywin, Eddard, and Robert most of the time, if only because Hoster Tully and Jon Arryn are already dead), and Dany's is even shorter. She also contains her revenge pretty well, which we see at Meereen, when she kills the

157 hostages as revenge for the slain children. At the point when she arrives in Westeros, no living participant other than Jaime will have been left. And she was always driven more by the desire to regain her throne than by avenging it, anyway – which is, of course, not to say that she wouldn't be sucked into a bloody struggle when the Martells start it. Obviously, Viserys talks a lot about taking revenge on those that betrayed him, and his initial reign would surely have been bloody with the heads of the main rebels. But imagine him winning pretty fast, with almost the whole of Westeros bending the knee – I can't see him starting a revenge-fueled killing spree. (That's not to say that he wouldn't later start to pull an Aerys and burn people to death, perhaps even justifying it with the rebellion, but that's something different entirely.)

Enough with the Targaryen apologies – let's have a last look at someone who tries to do it differently and see how that goes down. The Night's Watch fought the wildlings for (at least) centuries, and when their new commander, Lord Snow, suddenly starts to throw open the gates and admit all those wildlings south to settle the gift and man the castles, many black brothers are incredibly – and understandably – upset about it. Make a drinking game out of how often someone mentions that he would rather kill the wildlings than feed and clothe them in Jon's chapters in *A Dance with Dragons*, and you won't be able to finish the book because you'll be passed out on the floor. Most of the Night's Watch's brothers want nothing more than to kill the wildlings, or at least let them die beyond the Wall, because everyone knows *someone* who died fighting them (that the same is true for the wildlings, too, never seems to occur to them).

This urge for revenge is kept under control only by the stern orders of Jon and the even sterner example he made of Janos Slynt and his disobedience. But in the end, the thirst for revenge in most of the brothers gets the better of them, most tragically in the case of Jon Snow. When he receives the Pink Letter, all he can think of is to take revenge himself on Ramsay, a decision that can be described as a bad one easily enough. He doesn't even take proper time for preparations, only talking to Tormund for two hours before departing for Winterfell and to his doom.

Throughout the series, revenge is one of the strongest motivators that drives the characters, and for all those who make it their primary motivation, there is nothing but blood and grief down the road. I'm going to take a leap here and proclaim that this is, in fact, intentional; like the plight of the smallfolk that is depicted throughout the whole story, the futility of revenge is also an underlying theme, one never really breaking the narrative surface to jump in your face. There's yet to be a sequence like brother Meribald's monologue to spell it out for everyone, but it's clearly there. If you look at just how badly those with a strong desire for revenge fare, this bodes ill for the future prospects of the Martell conspiracy or, perhaps most poignantly, the development of Arya Stark.

# THE PRINCE IS RIDING

Rebutting the identity of – and the aim of the conspiracy around – Aegon Targaryen

Miles Schneiderman

*"Based on the above musings, I strongly believe that Illyrio decided to take advantage of events to crown his son king of Westeros as a Targaryen pretender."*

Alexander Smith, "The Prince That Illyrio Promised"

"The Prince That Illyrio Promised" is my favorite essay from the original *A Flight of Sorrows* because it postulated and analyzed a theory that I had never previously considered. Granted, the revelation that Aegon Targaryen, presumed dead after the sack of King's Landing, is actually alive and prepared to take back the Iron Throne is a relatively new one. There's been speculation for years that Aegon was swapped for a double as an infant in an attempt to preserve the royal line, largely because George R.R. Martin refused to confirm his death, but it wasn't until 2011's *A Dance with Dragons* that Aegon appeared in the flesh. As a result, serious analysis of this development took some time to get started, and Alexander Smith's essay represents the most thorough examination of Aegon's return to date.

After years upon years of the so-called "baby Aegon" theory refusing to die, some might think that his sudden appearance and equally sudden invasion of Westeros would have put all speculation to rest.  Instead, the lost Targaryen was immediately met with skepticism from fans, many of whom are utterly resolved in their belief that the boy is a fake.  Smith is one such skeptic, and his proposal for Aegon's true identity is compelling and, initially, convincing – when I first read it, I was swayed by his arguments.  However, after going over the evidence on both sides, I'm convinced there is no conclusive evidence to indicate that Aegon is Illyrio's son, nor even that the young prince is anything other than what he claims to be.

## The Pretender

In order to accept that Aegon is actually Illyrio's son, we must accept that Aegon is not actually Aegon.  In other words, we have to disbelieve the official story about his identity as relayed to us in *Dance with Dragons*.

Before continuing, it should be noted that Jon Connington, likely one of the only living characters who has seen both Rhaegar Targaryen and Aegon, believes they were father and son.  Furthermore, Varys seems to believe in Aegon's identity himself, as evidenced by his revelation to Kevan Lannister in the epilogue of *Dance*.  With Kevan dying and Pycelle dead, Varys has no obvious reason to lie.  Despite this, a large portion of the fanbase still believes that he is, indeed, lying, and Connington is being fooled.

There are three primary arguments in favor of Aegon being a pretender.  The first involves the writing tendencies of Martin, who, as Smith points out, is fond of giving his characters false or secret identities and has based several aspects of his story on a real historic event, the War of the Roses. These are real trends, and there's no going against them; Martin does love to cloak people under assumed names and guises, and there really was a pretender to the English throne named Perkin Warbeck. If Aegon is a fake, it would fit with Martin's style and coincide with British history.

That's all well and good, but it's hardly conclusive. Just because something has happened multiple times, it doesn't necessarily follow that it will happen again. While the correlations between real and Westerosi history are interesting and provide realism to the series, it remains a work of fantasy, and Martin is under no obligation to include his version of Perkin Warbeck. One might even argue that the "pretender to the throne" story has already been included, albeit indirectly, in the form of the Blackfyre Pretenders. While a fake Aegon would fit previous trends, this alone is not enough to cast serious doubt on his claim. Logic dictates that we look deeper.

The second argument against Aegon invokes that dreaded specter of speculation, prophecy. In the House of the Undying, Daenerys Targaryen has a brief vision: "A cloth dragon swayed on poles amidst a cheering crowd" (*A Clash of Kings*, Daenerys IV). Later, during one of her enigmatic warnings, Quaithe tells Dany about a host of individuals making their way to her, among them "the mummer's dragon" (*A Dance with Dragons*, Daenerys II). Taken together, these two clues point to a false Targaryen, a pretender who will be cheered by the people and taken for a dragon, the kind of trickery most often associated with the mummer's profession. A fake Aegon would certainly fit in this role.

Like the first argument, however, this one has the cart before the horse. Yes, Aegon might fit this particular interpretation of these prophetic visions, but he's under no obligation to do so. Indeed, there's absolutely no guarantee that the popular interpretation is the correct one. Martin has spent a lot of time in these books demonstrating the fickle nature of prophecy, and we cannot come to a conclusion about Aegon's identity simply because we think we know what "the mummer's dragon" means. There are a whole bunch of characters out there who may or may not be secret Targaryens: Jon Snow, Tyrion Lannister, even Varys. The vision could refer to any of these, or none. It need not even mean a false Targaryen pretending to be a real one – Smith points out the connection between Varys and mummery to support Aegon's falsehood, but doesn't this just mean the prophecy is that much more likely to refer to Varys himself? Moreover, why would Quaithe warn Dany of the coming of the mummer's dragon if the dragon in question isn't anywhere near her, and won't be any time soon? If that's prophecy, Quaithe is bad at it, and Tyrion has the power to thwart the hand of fate with his big mouth.

I bring these examples and possibilities up merely to illustrate that prophecy makes for an unsound leg to stand on. We can't confirm any of them until they have already been fulfilled. As Stefan Sasse wrote in his essay "Under the Bleeding Star," "For good or for ill, we are bound to interpret and misinterpret [prophecies] as the characters do themselves and, thus, experience the struggle for knowledge firsthand." Dany's visions and Quaithe's warnings are insufficient evidence against Aegon's Targaryen blood.

The third argument is a major part of Smith's essay and involves analyzing what we know of Varys's and Illyrio's plan to restore the Targaryen dynasty.   Smith says Illyrio does not possess enough of a motive to place a Targaryen on the throne, demonstrated by how little he has to gain, his treatment of Dany and Viserys, and the problematic nature of the original plan to storm the Seven Kingdoms with a Dothraki horde. This line of thinking also lends itself to questioning Aegon's true origins; if Varys and Illyrio had a ready-made Targaryen heir hidden away, why bother with the other two?  And if you are going to bother with the other two, why treat Aegon like the prince he is while abandoning his aunt and uncle to a mean life of squalor and disrepute?   While these questions are legitimate, they can also be satisfactorily answered.

### The Plan

Smith's biggest problem with the plan is that it relies so heavily on the Dothraki.  However, thanks to *A Feast for Crows* and *A Dance with Dragons*, we now know that was never going to be the case.  It wasn't going to be just the Dothraki – it was going to be them alongside the Golden Company (via Aegon and Jon Connington) and Dorne (via Arianne Martell).

Here's how it would have worked:   Illyrio sells Daenerys for Khal Drogo's allegiance, while Viserys is kept on hand to marry Arianne and ensure the allegiance of Dorne, which we know thanks to Prince Doran's words in *Feast for Crows*. (Remember, Viserys was never supposed to go with his sister across the Dothraki Sea.)   Illyrio clearly expected Drogo to fulfill his part of the bargain eventually (see the secret conversation between him and Varys, overheard by Arya Stark in *A Game of Thrones*), and Tristan Rivers, a captain of the Golden Company, makes it clear in *Dance* that Viserys and the Dothraki were supposed to join up with the sellswords for the invasion.   The allegiance of the Golden Company itself is acquired through Varys's pact with Myles Toyne and Jon Connington.   Theoretically, then, when the time was right, Viserys and Aegon would join forces, leading the combined strength of the Dothraki, the Golden Company, and Dorne.   The Golden Company, we know, fields 10,000 swords, plus certain weapons and tactics that give them an advantage, such as elephants.   Drogo had 40,000 mounted warriors in his *khalasar* (true, Viserys talks about taking the Seven Kingdoms with only 10,000, but he was an idiot, and there's no reason to believe the Dothraki wouldn't bring more).   The strength of Dorne isn't exactly known; while they are the weakest major house in Westeros in terms of military power, they would certainly add *something* to this already considerable host.

In *Game of Thrones*, Varys tells Ned Stark that he was desperate to keep Robert Baratheon alive.   Indeed, how could he not have been?   Had King Robert been on the throne when the Targaryens came across the sea with their allies, he would have met them in combat regardless of the odds or the tenets of strategy.   Jorah Mormont admits to Daenerys that, while the Dothraki have no taste for siegecraft, Robert is enough of a fool to fight them on the open field.   Mormont also describes his perspective on how that fight would go:

> *"When I first went into exile, I looked at the Dothraki and saw half-naked barbarians, as wild as their horses. If you*

*had asked me then, Princess, I should have told you that a thousand good knights would have no trouble putting to flight a hundred times as many Dothraki. "*

*"But if I asked you now?"*

*"Now," the knight said, "I am less certain. They are better riders than any knight, utterly fearless, and their bows outrange ours... The Dothraki fire from horseback, charging or retreating, it makes no matter, they are full as deadly... and there are so many of them, my lady... How long do you imagine [common Westerosi soldiers] would stand against a charge of forty thousand screamers howling for blood? How well would boiled leather jerkins and mailed shirts protect them when the arrows fall like rain?"*

*A Game of Thrones,* Daenerys IV

With this in mind, consider the plan as it must have looked originally. Aegon and Viserys arrive with an army. Between the Golden Company, the Dothraki, and the Dornish, we're talking about at least 30,000 warriors here, and that's the low end – the high end is more like 60,000. Do the math. This army is huge, and as soon as the war begins, houses will start defecting back to the Targaryens left and right. Aegon is by now the most eligible bachelor in the Seven Kingdoms; he marries Margaery Tyrell or Lysa Arryn or even Cersei Lannister to secure the loyalty of one of the major houses. The picture you're looking at here is a picture of a restored Targaryen dynasty.

Meanwhile, Illyrio's ambivalence toward the fate of the two Targaryens, Daenerys and Viserys, also makes sense. Dany doesn't need to survive the Dothraki Sea – she only has to be sold. If she gives the khal a son before she perishes, so much the better, but the price for Drogo's army has been paid. Her role in the scheme is vital, but small; before her dragons hatched, she didn't appear to be a major part of anyone's invasion plans. Viserys might have had a bigger part, but not by much. Of all these alliances, Dorne is the one that would take the least work. Doran Martell has been in something of a vengeful mood for a long time now; the planned marriage between Viserys and Arianne would have helped seal things, but it isn't nearly as important as Dany's marriage to Drogo or the pact between Varys, Toyne, and Connington. Viserys brings the least to the table with his marriage, and it was Illyrio, not Viserys, who made the agreement with Khal Drogo. So, yes, when Viserys defies his handlers and wanders off with the Dothraki, Illyrio blinks for a moment and lets him go. With Aegon alive and the Dornish likely allies regardless, Viserys is pretty much expendable.

Why did Illyrio wait years before even appearing to care about Dany and Viserys instead of immediately taking them in? First, because Aegon is the Man. He gets the training, he gets the learning, he's the one preparing to be king, he gets hidden away and protected. Viserys and Daenerys are useful pawns for bringing in their respective alliances, but they remain ever secondary. Aegon is the heir. And while his continued existence is a tightly-kept secret, the Iron Throne keeps tabs on Viserys and Dany throughout their lives. In fact, Varys is the very person who does that job. Why let the last Targaryens live in poverty and allow Viserys to gain himself the moniker of the Beggar King? So that the world knows what the Targaryens have been reduced to, thus removing suspicion that they will rise again. See every Ned Stark quote from every conversation with Robert in which Daenerys comes up for examples of this.

Moreover, Viserys is on board with Illyrio's plans right from the beginning of their association, an eagerness that has to stem, at least in part, from somebody finally taking him in and promising him the throne. Sheltering the two young Targaryens from an early age would probably have been an even better means of securing their compliance, but the fact is that Dany and Viserys were known to be alive and were being spied on. If word had gotten out that the children were being sheltered by Illyrio Mopatis, he would have been cast into a very suspicious light. No one knew about Aegon, though. By keeping the hidden Targaryen out of sight and ignoring the other two, Varys and Illyrio were able to hatch their plans while King Robert's eyes were elsewhere. They were able to make key moves in the game of thrones without anyone realizing they were playing.

The first argument against Aegon relies on patterns, not evidence. The second argument rests on the shaky ground of prophecy and dream. The third falls apart when the true plan comes to light. As of right now, there is very little to suggest that Aegon Targaryen is a pretender.

### The Progeny

That said, let's pretend for a moment that he is. After all, just because there's no firm evidence for it, it doesn't necessarily make it false. Aegon could still turn out to be a pretender. Could he turn out to be Illyrio's son, though?

Smith makes several interesting points when discussing this possibility. He reminds us that Illyrio's second wife, who had golden hair streaked with silver, was of the slave class, and that Illyrio found himself lower in status after marrying her. Smith speculates that Pentos might not be the best place for the son of a slave woman and a tarnished magister to grow up. He suggests that Illyrio must be motivated by more than just gold, that he wants a better life for his son – a better life that will be found on the seat of the Iron Throne. Smith points out the fact that Illyrio seems to know Aegon well, and to possess a great deal of affection for the boy, reinforcing the notion that Aegon might actually be Illyrio's progeny.

First things first: none of the speculation regarding how the good people of Pentos would have treated Illyrio's son by his second wife can be in any way confirmed. We don't know how much stigma would be attached due to a slave background in the city; to be frank, we don't know all that much about Pentos, period. That said, after all the lavish descriptions of his fabulous wealth, it would be a great surprise to me to learn that the son of a man like Magister Illyrio would be allowed to grow up in anything other than comfort.

Additionally, there's no need to invent a father-son relationship to explain Illyrio's attachment to Aegon or his core motivations. It seems probable that Aegon, son or no, spent his early years with Illyrio. We know that he was born approximately 17 years ago; we know that Jon Connington left the Golden Company 12 years ago. Even if the transition from mansion to pole boat was immediate (unlikely, but possible), that still leaves five years of Illyrio taking care of Aegon, probably with visits in the years between. This explains Illyrio's apparent affection for the boy without necessitating a blood bond.

Illyrio's true motives are unclear, just as the true motives of Varys are unclear. But the lure of gold for a man like Illyrio Mopatis should not be brushed aside just because he has a lot of gold already. Rich men can *never* have enough; the dearest desire of a person with a lot of money is to acquire more money. Illyrio's greed is his defining characteristic. Smith wonders why he would get involved in happenings across the narrow sea, proclaiming, "He already has enough wealth and power in his native city to satisfy any man." That statement, however, does not apply to Illyrio. Why does this man want more wealth and power? Because there's more to be had.

If Illyrio has personal reasons for getting involved, they relate to Varys, not Aegon. It's certainly possible, given the previous point about Aegon's childhood, that Illyrio has come to think of him as a son and, thus, would welcome his rise to power. Still, if that's the case, it strikes me as a secondary motive, not a primary one. Aegon grew up in Illyrio's house because Illyrio had plans for him, not the other way around.

Thus far, the hardest evidence we have suggests that Aegon's father was indeed Rhaegar Targaryen, Prince of Dragonstone. Maybe later we'll find out that he is an imposter, and why and how he was made into a false claimant for the throne. Until then, we might want to start thinking about the fact that the second head of the dragon has landed an army on the shores of Westeros.

# A FEAST OF VIPERS

*Ethnic diversity, personal identification, and
fandom theories in Dorne*

Amin Javadi

Dorne is my favorite region in the Seven
Kingdoms of Westeros, and House Manwoody is a
microcosm of a lot of what is great about Dorne.
Their house seat, Kingsgrave, is a symbol of past
defiance and badassery, where an enemy king
invading Dorne was killed. The name Manwoody is
a tongue-in-cheek joke by George R.R. Martin, but
it still reflects the greater sexual liberty in Dorne
itself. Their house symbol, the crowned skull, is
just one of many great Dornish banners,
culminating in the majestic sun and spear of the
Martells. It is definitely worth examining how
George has managed to make Dorne such a
popular place for both A Podcast of Ice and Fire
and much of the fandom in general.

Dorne does not debut in the spotlight at
the beginning of the series. *A Game of Thrones* is
heavily focused on the growing conflict between
the Starks and the Lannisters, with the Baratheons
caught in between. It is heavily skewed toward
King's Landing, and there is no one of Dornish
background mentioned at court, save for the
master-at-arms, Ser Aron Santagar, who is dead by
the middle of *A Clash of Kings*. The lack of a
Dornish presence is no surprise in hindsight, given

the icy relations between the Crown and the Prince of Dorne during Robert's reign.   But the lack of participation in the plot doesn't diminish its foreshadowing; the faint hints and glimmers of something greater to come hang over the entire first book.

(The same is true with *Game of Thrones*, which similarly features an early focus on the Starks, Lannisters, and their more closely related houses.[1]   HBO's adaptation, however, does a laudable job of consistent Dornish name-dropping without overdoing it.   Given this, it is likely that the absence of the term "Rhoynar" in season one was a simple omission to help the pilot flow more freely rather than an attempt to drop the Rhoynar element entirely from the TV show, since they form such an important part of the Dornish equation.[2])

Dorne's role in the series slowly grows in *A Clash of Kings*.   The Martells are mentioned as a force to be reckoned with by Renly Baratheon, among others.    Tyrion Lannister specifically targets Prince Doran in his negotiations to help the Lannisters win a war on many fronts.   Princess Myrcella Baratheon is sent to the southern kingdom to be betrothed to Prince Trystane, accompanied by her sworn shield and knight of the Kingsguard, Ser Arys Oakheart.

This last development in particular touches on what proves to be one of the most important

---

[1] The focus on the Starks and Lannisters is taken to the point of reducing House Tyrell's total mustering strength to third place, after those two houses.

[2] "King of the Rhoynar" is not mentioned as one of Robert's titles during Eddard's execution of the Night's Watch deserter in episode 101.

buried storylines of the overarching story: the Lannister-Martell blood feud. Marriage pacts, like the fostering of children, have been used as attempts to end feuds in the past. This has had various results, from the failure of the Bracken/Blackwood peaces to the successful addition of Dorne to a united Westeros under Targaryen rule.[3] Tyrion likely hoped that this betrothal could help end the conflict, and we are not given the Dornish perspective on the matter until much later in the series.

It is in *A Storm of Swords* that Dorne jumps to the forefront, accompanying the dash of Oberyn Martell to the front of the narrative and into a popular place in fandom. If Manwoody is a house that well represents Dorne, the Red Viper is an individual who reflects much of what Dorne is. Oberyn is intelligent and witty, skilled at battle and in the bedroom. He is open and free with his relationships but takes care of all his children born from his dalliances, and he has a loving relationship with his paramour, Ellaria Sand. Oberyn also represents some of the potential vices of Dorne, in particular a bit of the rashness, thirst for revenge, and the hot Dornish temper that is referred to several times in the series, including in the song about the Dornishman's wife. Later on in the books, we meet his brother, Doran, who shows the other side of Dorne: the necessary diplomacy, manipulation, and long-term planning. Doran, in his own words, is "the grass that hides the viper from his enemies and shelters him until he

---

[3] The Bracken/Blackwood dispute was outlined in detail in *A Dance with Dragons*, with a mention of several past marriages and peace agreements. (See *A Dance with Dragons*, Jaime I.) Interestingly, the princess involved in the peace marriage with Dorne was named Daenerys, daughter of Aegon IV.

strikes."[4]  But in *Storm*, we are treated solely to Oberyn, whose interactions at King's Landing, particularly with Tyrion, form much of the best parts of the third and best book in the series.

During *Storm of Swords*, we learn more about the Lannister-Martell feud and how the Martells once bested Tywin in the field of marriage proposals, and how Tywin may have taken his revenge for that lost tilt with the murder of Elia and her children.  It is a testament to Martin's grey writing that we are not particularly sure if Tywin intentionally gave the order for Elia to be killed; Tywin denies it and instead claims that the children were killed only for political reasons, while Oberyn believes otherwise.  We hear the Red Viper brazenly talking about Dornish plans to crown Myrcella, without caring about what little birds or spiders may be listening to his words; Oberyn is secure in both his personal abilities and his political protections as a younger prince of Dorne.  It is a shock to both him and the readers to see his aura of invincibility savagely crushed by the smoldering gauntlet of Ser Gregor Clegane.  Dornish vengeance would have to wait for Doran's long game rather than the Red Viper's quick strike, though Oberyn would at least ensure the apparent demise of Ser Gregor with the use of his poisoned spear.[5]  Oberyn may have succeeded in taking down Tywin with poison as well, if you believe a theory followed by some members of the fandom.[6]

---

[4] *A Dance with Dragons*, The Watcher.

[5] There is quite a bit of evidence that Gregor has been resurrected in some form as Ser Robert Strong. However, it is quite possible that Gregor has lost his own personality, whatever little was there in the first place, as well as his free will.

[6] See the post "Tywin Lannister: Dead Man Shitting?" at All

Dorne is one of the central locations in *A Feast for Crows*, where we finally get a glimpse of the inner working of the Dornish court, generally, and the reaction to Prince Oberyn's death, specifically. The diverse Sand Snakes are a reflection both of Oberyn's legacy and of the unique status of women in that region. Nowhere but in Dorne can we imagine such a motley band of bastard daughters able to wield this level of influence and be considered enough of a threat to Doran to warrant being taken under custody. We also learn more about the remainder of the Martell family, primarily Arianne and her father, Doran. The two are ambiguous characters, and fans have interpreted their actions in various ways. Some praise Doran's long-term planning, while others criticize him for being overcautious and too slow to act. It is definitely possible to do both, and Doran and the rest of the Dornish court are definitely interesting, well-rounded characters that add a bit of (Dornish) spice to the story. One of the strongest moments in *Feast* is Doran's "blood and fire" reveal, and his reconciliation with Arianne.

After years of waiting for *A Dance with Dragons*, we finally witnessed firsthand the last member of the immediate Martell family, Quentyn. Doran's son was in some ways not only a disappointment to Daenerys Targaryen, but also to a legion of Dornish fans that were eagerly waiting to see another Prince Oberyn and encountered the Frog instead. Perhaps they had unreasonably high expectations that were amplified by the wait for the fifth book.

I personally liked Quentyn, and it was sorry to see him reach his painfully extended demise.

---

Leather Must Be Boiled.

He shouldered the heavy weight of his father's and Dornish expectations and eventually buckled underneath the pressure. We shall never surely know if his Targaryen blood would have been enough to tame a dragon, but it was a valiant effort – even if foolhardy. Quentyn's own legacy may be in the twisted stories of his demise that will surely reach Dorne and may taint the potential support Dany could have expected there. Other than the Vale of Arryn, Dorne is the only major region of Westeros to not have been bloodied by the War of the Five Kings, and it will certainly play a large role in the future.

It is Dorne's unique nature in the Seven Kingdoms that is a major reason why it is a fan favorite in the series, and part of this unique nature lies in its ethnic diversity. Tyrion describes the three major groups of people in Dorne:

> There were the salty Dornishmen who lived along the coasts, the sandy Dornishmen of the deserts and long river valleys, and the stony Dornishmen who made their fastnesses in the passes and heights of the Red Mountains. The salty Dornishmen had the most Rhoynish blood, the stony Dornishmen the least. All three sorts seemed well represented in Doran's retinue. The salty Dornishmen were lithe and dark, with smooth olive skin and long black hair streaming in the wind. The sandy Dornishmen were even darker, their faces burned brown by the hot Dornish sun. They wound long bright scarves around their helms to ward off sunstroke. The stony Dornishmen were biggest and fairest, sons of the Andals and the First Men, brown-haired or blond, with faces

*that freckled or burned in the sun instead
of browning.*

*A Storm of Swords*, Tyrion V

There is a lot to take away from this
description and our later knowledge of Dorne.
One fact is the general ethnic diversity of the
kingdom, which we can suspect is also echoed by
a variety of cultural traditions present there. We
know that there are still followers of the Rhoynish
religion present along with the Faith of the Seven,
without any apparent conflict (so far), despite the
hardening of religious lines in other, more war-
torn areas of Westeros.

We know that the Yronwoods have had a
lot of strife with the Martells in the past, taking
different sides in various rebellions and conflicts.
Perhaps a difference in ethnicity played a role, as
the Yronwoods may be more of Andal stock or
have less Rhoynish blood due to their location
near the Boneway. However, it seems that the
most recent conflict had more to do with personal
disagreements and duels than anything with the
color of Yronwood and Martell skin. It is
refreshing that their differences in ethnic
background haven't been stressed, and it is more
the Yronwoods' past strength as one of the
historic kings in Dorne and the relative
geographical distances between the two houses
that are probably the main source of the enduring
rivalry. It is a testament to Doran's diplomacy
that he was able to heal the current generation's
blood feud with the fostering of his son, Quentyn.
Depending on the strength of that upbringing and
the connections forged between the two families,
it may be the united outrage over Quentyn's death
that helps keep Yronwood and Martell on the same
side in the hardships soon to come.

To use a term quite anachronistic to *A Song of Ice and Fire*, Dorne is in some ways a multicultural state, and a surprisingly successful one, at that. This is indicated by the fair representation and diversity present in the retinue sent with Oberyn to King's Landing. It is also reflected in the Water Gardens, where children of all ranks and backgrounds are able to play together, from commoner to prince and princess.[7] It may be that external conflicts with the rest of Westeros – first the Reach and the Stormlands, then, later, the Targaryens – helped keep this disparate amalgamation of peoples together and form the unique Dornish identity. "[B]lood, custom, geography, and history all helped to set the Dornishmen apart from the other kingdoms," and it is this Dornish identity that may have fuelled their intense resistance to Targaryen attacks.[8]

Dorne, in fact, was the sole kingdom of Westeros to continually and successfully resist Aegon's conquest. "Unbowed, Unbent, Unbroken" are the Martell house words, but they can apply equally to the whole of Dorne, which learned from the mistakes of the other, kneeling kings and avoided fighting the Targaryen war machine head-on. Instead, they resorted to (and perhaps invented) guerrilla warfare tactics, making the most of their lower numbers and taking full advantage of their country's natural terrain and landscape. The complete details of Dorne's successful resistance against Targaryen dragons have not been revealed yet, but hopefully we will learn more about it in the future, as it may be relevant to present conflicts involving Dany. (It is interesting to note that the Rhoynar who settled

---

[7] *A Dance with Dragons,* The Watcher.
[8] *A Dance with Dragons,* appendix, House Martell entry.

in Dorne initially fled Essos due to Valyrian aggression and expansion; the struggle between Dorne and the Iron Throne was, in a way, a variation on that theme. The past history may have particularly inspired Dornish resistance and a "this far, and no further" attitude.)

We hear from several contemporary characters about the historic temporary conquest of Dorne by the Young Dragon. Daeron I Targaryen sent an overwhelming force to take the last kingdom, utilizing naval superiority to attack by both land and sea. The youth wrote about his victory in a work titled *The Conquest of Dorne*, exaggerating the Dornish numbers he faced. Daeron's control over Dorne, of course, would not last, and he and thousands of his men would perish during the Dornish uprising. The Red Viper best describes the source and spread of this successful rebellion:

> When the Young Dragon conquered Dorne so long ago, he left the Lord of Highgarden to rule us after the Submission of Sunspear. This Tyrell moved with his tail from keep to keep, chasing rebels and making certain that our knees stayed bent. He would arrive in force, take a castle for his own, stay a moon's turn, and ride on to the next castle. It was his custom to turn the lords out of their own chambers and take their beds for himself. One night, he found himself beneath a heavy velvet canopy. A sash hung down near the pillows, should he wish to summon a wench. He had a taste for Dornish women, this Lord Tyrell, and who can blame him? So he pulled upon the sash, and when he did, the canopy above him split open, and a hundred red scorpions fell down upon his

> *head. His death lit a fire that soon swept across Dome, undoing all the Young Dragon's victories in a fortnight. The kneeling men stood up, and we were free again.*

*A Storm of Swords*, Tyrion IX

Dorne's eventual peaceful addition to Targaryen rule allowed them to keep their distinct cultural identity that has proven to be so popular amongst fandom. Primarily amongst the customs inherited from the Rhoynar is the strong status of women in Dorne in regards to dynastic succession as well as sexual freedom. Dorne as a whole seems more sexually relaxed than the remainder of the kingdoms, with accepted paramours and the bending of the usual Andal traditions like the chastity requirements of the Kingsguard. This makes Dorne more directly appealing to 21$^{st}$ century readers, because even if we accept the "standards of the time" argument, it is still hard for some readers to parse through the greater misogyny present in the rest of Westeros.

Beyond the sex, it is the exotic setting of Dorne that catches the reader's eye. From fiery Dornish peppers to blood oranges to possibly feathered hats, Dorne just seems like a livelier and more fun place to visit, compared to the rest of the kingdoms. "Never drink with Dornishmen when the moon is full" is the old Westerosi adage, but I suspect many people in fandom would like to do just that.[9]

Dorne injects zest and piquancy into the series not dissimilar to the effect of the spices and luxuries brought back to the West as a result of

---

[9] *A Dance with Dragons*, Jon XIII.

the Crusades. It is not surprising that Dorne's real-world inspiration has been speculated by the fandom to be a blend of medieval Spain, North Africa, and the Middle East. There have been vigorous debates on exactly where to place the kingdom, but it is important to keep in mind that Dorne, like the rest of the story, is not a one-to-one transition from our world to Martin's. George himself has noted how boring it would be to have direct parallels for both characters and locations, and it is mainly the inspirations of various sources that aid him in his splendid worldbuilding. George specifically mentioned Wales, Palestine, and the Moorish conquest of Spain as being useful inspirations for creating Dorne. (The various placements of Dorne have been reflected in the vast quantity of art, both official and fan-made, which has produced Dornish castles, vistas, and characters that vary in range from Southern European to Middle Eastern.)

It is George's worldbuilding that has particularly made Dorne my own favorite place in Westeros. I like that George created a spectrum of ethnicities that many of us can personally identify with. Given that much of North Africa and the Middle East are currently behind the rest of the world on issues like women's rights and sexual freedoms, it is refreshing to see Martin avoid a potential stereotype with Dorne and turn our potential expectations on their heads, just as he has already subverted so many classical fantasy tropes.

HBO now has a chance to follow Martin's path in casting the Dornish in the upcoming few seasons of *Game of Thrones*. As said, there is a lot of room for variety here, and many casting choices could be justified one way or another with the textual references present in the books. It is my hope that they do pick some of the more ethnically diverse actors for the Martells (Alexander Siddig being one of my dream choices) and at least some of the other Dornish characters, as it would be a more faithful representation of the books.   Unlike Qarth and some of the other casting done, Dorne does have an inherent diversity of skin colors and can be HBO's best chance to upturn TV tropes and stereotypes.

Whatever the choice, though, I do look forward to seeing more of Dorne on-screen – and in the spotlight – in the TV show.

## Epilogue in Sunspear

I wrote this essay some time before the press release of HBO's casting Pedro Pascal for Prince Oberyn Martell was released.  While Pascal did fit within the canonical range of casting for Dorne, there was a debate in the fandom that resulted in some comments from George on how he had pictured the "salty" Dornishmen on his LiveJournal, specifically more as Mediterranean (Southern European).[10]

There is too much to cover here, but there are a few points that are worth making.  First of all, it appeared that some in the fandom had given George too much credit in the construction of Dorne.   I thought he was subverting expectations about North Africa and the Middle East[11]; others thought he was subverting the idea of racial categorization with the description

---

[10] See the post "We're Number One...," dated June 29th, 2013, at grrm.livejournal.com.

[11] Though this may still be possible in terms of the "sandy" Dornishmen, as George's comment on them was far briefer and could use some clarification on whether he meant to distinguish or include them in his review.

written down by the conquering Targaryens that matched what past conquerors had done.[12]

One could take the background context into consideration and debate whether George was influenced by a desire to back up Pedro Pascal (who did not himself deserve any criticism) and the TV show. This might explain the contrast between his recent statement and some of his past statements and the descriptions in the text. However, the better option is to take George at his word and consider what that means for fan interpretations of Dorne. This path boils down to the realization that authors do not have complete control over how their work is interpreted – nor should they. Canonical text descriptions as well as the vast multitude of art, both official and fan-made, supported a wide spectrum of interpretations for Dorne.[13] This variety should not be quashed, even by authorial decree, which, in fact, isn't what happened. George understood the reality of personal interpretation: "The picture in the author's head and the picture in the reader's head don't always match, and, really, there's no reason they should. That's one of the great things about books. The reader is part of the process. No two readers see the character the same way."[14]

As for the TV show, there is one comment in a discussion I took part in, covering Dornish casting suggestions, that I want to respond to.

---

[12] See the Fat Pink Cast on Tumblr.

[13] I own *The Art of Ice and Fire* (volumes I and II), as well as the *Game of Thrones* board and card games. They are officially licensed through Fantasy Flight Games and contain a wide variety of Dornish interpretations, from the characters to the architecture.

[14] See the post "We're Number One...," dated June 29th, 2013, at grrm.livejournal.com.

Others and I were accused of "only identifying with people who are the same skin color and being defined by skin color" rather than "personality, motivations, or worldview." I thought this was an intentionally baiting comment, but it is still worth exploring. Obviously, there are multiple grounds for identifying with people, and we all identify with characters of different ethnic backgrounds, genders, sexual orientations, and so forth, so we don't only identify by skin color. In fact, we identify with people, both in fiction and in history, based on a variety of reasons, including those described.

However, it is undeniable that in reading texts and watching visual media, there is an impact of seeing someone who looks like you, particularly when the majority of these portrayals are still steeped in stereotypes and caricatures – and that's if they even appear at all. When placed in this specific context, a more complex interpretation (whether positive or not) is preferred and enjoyed. Dorne, after all, has both its strengths and vices, but it is neither simplistic nor stereotypical. It is this drive for complexity that will continue to fuel fandom interpretations of Dorne and the rest of Martin's *A Song of Ice and Fire*.

# THE KING'S JUSTICE IS MUTE, NOT BLIND

*Why trials in Westeros are not what they seem*

John Jasmin

Cersei Lannister once said, "If the wicked do not fear the King's Justice, you have put the wrong man in the office." The King's Justice is, of course, best known for one responsibility: the execution of those who have been condemned by the king. Unlike the master of coin, who oversees a band of tax collectors, or the master of whispers, who manages a network of spies, the King's Justice is a one-man office. He does not have deputies dispatching heads throughout the kingdom. He makes no laws, issues no warrants, and sets no bounties. And, most significantly, the King's Justice does not need to be convinced of crime or guilt. The actual trials and sentencings are left to others, so it's understandable that most people cower when the single-minded Justice nears.

The king's justice, on the other hand, is something that most people see as necessary and good. At its core, the king's justice is about upholding the king's laws and punishing those who violate them. But is that any different from regular justice? Surely the king's justice cannot be subject to what the current king decides is fair. Jaehaerys the Conciliator's notion of justice was undoubtedly benevolent, but woe be to the man who had to defend himself to Maegor the Cruel.  And before he devolved into the Mad King, Aerys II was said to be charming and generous; a crime perpetrated late in his reign likely faced a different brand of justice than the same crime committed earlier.

It is no small irony that the man who would eventually become the King's Justice received a firsthand account of how arbitrarily punitive the king's justice can be.  Ser Ilyn Payne once boasted that it was Tywin Lannister, the Hand of the King, who ruled the Seven Kingdoms, not the king.  For this offense, the Mad King had Ilyn's tongue ripped out with hot pincers.  He never had a chance to defend himself.  Then again, what Ilyn claimed was not true, and the punishment confirmed it as a lie; a man who held all of the realm's power would not have stood by powerlessly, as Tywin did, while the king mutilated the commander of his guard for a perceived slight.  Here we have another instance of how the system of laws in Westeros is lacking, as the concepts of punishment and trial are sometimes interchangeable, and they seldom lead to actual justice.

### Punishments and the Right to a Trial

The penalties for committing crimes in Westeros are well known:  thieves lose a hand, rapists are gelded, and murderers dangle from a noose.  The severity of these punishments makes for a strong deterrent.  What makes an even stronger deterrent is their absolutism.  For all its problems investigating crimes and identifying culprits, Westeros is clear on this.  Once a man has been accused of a crime, punishment is a foregone conclusion. Guilt isn't irrelevant – it's presumed.

Aside from fleeing into exile, one alternative allows the accused to avoid the more common penalties of his crime: he can join the Night's Watch. That is a punishment of its own. A man of the Night's Watch is guaranteed a lifetime of servitude in a harsh climate. He cannot hold lands or raise a family, and he forfeits his life should he ever desert. But his past crimes are forgiven when he takes the black, and the only risk of losing limbs there is from frostbite. The Night's Watch can be remedial, too, though not by reforming a conscripted man so that he can contribute later to society. Rather, the trades and skills he develops as a black brother are for the good of the Night's Watch itself. They may even help him advance to positions of genuine authority within the brotherhood. Despite all its challenges, the Night's Watch is one of the few meritocracy-based societies that Westeros has. As far as second chances go, life on the Wall isn't half bad.

Still, submitting to corporal punishment or taking the black can be seen as an admission of guilt. The system may not particularly care about this, but the accused might. He will always carry with him the stigma of the crime, guilty or innocent. Even on the Wall, where a man can remake himself, an alleged murderer or rapist is often regarded as inferior to those who joined the Night's Watch with honor.

So if the accused maintains his innocence, it seems obvious that he should demand a trial. But it's not so evident that everyone in Westeros has that option. Whereas any man, regardless of station, may submit to punishment or take the black, we've witnessed few instances of a trial where the alleged perpetrator wasn't of noble birth. When a commoner is brought before the king's justice, he is dealt with summarily. Perhaps no one will listen to his protestations of innocence. Perhaps he has no witnesses who will speak to his defense. It's more likely that because everyone in Westeros is presumed guilty, the lord adjudicating the case sees no value in a lengthy trial on behalf of a guilty commoner.

The highborn are presumed guilty, too, even if they're more successful in delaying punishment than the common folk. Remember how Tyrion Lannister was accused of attempting to kill Bran Stark? Lady Catelyn Stark declared, in a room full of allies, "In the name of King Robert and the good lords you serve, I call upon you to seize [Tyrion] and help me return him to Winterfell to await the king's justice." That's all it took to get Tyrion into her custody. Catelyn ended up bringing him to the Eyrie, where he was promptly tossed into the dungeon. He was not offered a chance to prove his innocence, and he spent many cold nights gazing out from the notorious sky cells. Catelyn had a dagger as evidence of Tyrion's guilt, but she dared not kill him outright without risking a war between the Starks and the Lannisters.

That's the great advantage of nobility here, and one that similarly kept Lord Eddard Stark and Ser Davos Seaworth alive during their respective days as an alleged traitor and a would-be murderer. Like Tyrion, neither Eddard nor Davos were offered an audience with the kings they betrayed, let alone a trial to defend themselves. Like Tyrion, neither could be punished for practical reasons even though they (unlike Tyrion) were undeniably guilty.

What got Eddard and Tyrion out of their dungeons was their eventual willingness to confess. Eddard's admission of guilt led to his

immediate execution.   Tyrion was more clever.
Before the entirety of the Eyrie's court, Tyrion
confessed to all manner of sins, but not to the
charges leveled at him:   "You accuse me of
crimes, I deny them, so you throw me into an
open cell to freeze and starve.   Where is the
king's justice?  Is the Eyrie not part of the Seven
Kingdoms?  I stand accused, you say. Very well.  I
demand a trial!  Let me speak, and let my truth or
falsehood be judged openly, in the sight of gods
and men."

### At the Mercy of Men

Tyrion Lannister is the subject of the two
biggest trials of the series to date, so his
experiences provide the basis for our
understanding of the Westerosi court system.  We
know Tyrion to be innocent of the crimes of which
he was accused, although his unguarded wit
sometimes made it hard to defend his innocence.
When Catelyn brought Tyrion to answer for an
attempt on her son's life, Lysa Arryn was quick to
add her lord husband's murder to the charges.
"Oh, did I kill him, too?" Tyrion responded, to no
one's amusement.  Joffrey's corpse was still warm
when Cersei Lannister demanded Tyrion arrested
for poisoning.  She later recounted a warning from
Tyrion that had seemingly come to pass:  "A day
will come when you think yourself safe and happy,
and suddenly your joy will turn to ashes in your
mouth, and you'll know the debt is paid."   Had
Tyrion been more banal and less quotable with his
threats, perhaps he would not have precluded in
his accusers' minds any reasonable doubt.
Once an accusation has been made and a
trial granted, the accused has a few options.  The
first is for the defendant to confront his accusers

before a local lord or tribunal. Sometimes the lord can be merciful. Eddard Stark articulated this when arguing against the practice of separating judges from executioners: "We hold to the belief that the man who passes the sentence should swing the sword." This isn't meant to dignify the final moments of the condemned; after all, Eddard would not have been consoled at his own beheading had Joffrey personally done the deed, and Farlen the kennelmaster would have suffered less had he not insisted on Theon Greyjoy's inexpert swings for his. Instead, Eddard's beliefs demanded absolute confidence before exacting justice. "If you would take a man's life," Eddard elaborated, "you owe it to him to look into his eyes and hear his final words. And if you cannot bear to do that, then perhaps the man does not deserve to die."

Sometimes the ruling lord can be honest. Storm's End survived a lengthy siege thanks to a practiced smuggler sneaking onions into the castle. As a result, Davos lost his fingers and gained a knighthood. "It was justice," Stannis Baratheon told the Onion Knight. "A good act does not wash out the bad, nor a bad act, the good. Each should have its own reward. You were a hero and a smuggler."

But most who stand accused aren't lucky enough to be judged by someone either merciful or honest. Tyrion recognized this, both in the Eyrie and in King's Landing. His fate would have been decided, respectively, by a little lord who wanted to make the "bad man" fly out the fiendish Moon Door, and by his lord father who admitted that he must judge Tyrion more harshly because he could not show favoritism toward his son (amusing, since Tywin Lannister spent so much effort insisting that Tyrion was no son of his). Facing no other recourse, Tyrion ultimately endured three days of a trial in King's Landing, in which Cersei brought forth dozens of witnesses who spouted truths, half-truths, and lies about his deviousness. Tyrion had no witnesses to refute Cersei's claims, and his guilt and subsequent condemnation were all but assured.

The accused has a second option: a trial by combat. It is said that the gods favor the man with the just cause, though often that turns out to be the man with the surest sword. And Tyrion understood perfectly well that those men are also more easily manipulated than lordly judges. With the promise of a substantial reward, he convinced Bronn to defend him in the Eyrie. The sellsword did just that, defeating Ser Vardis Egen with speed and guile. In King's Landing, Tyrion found an unlikely champion in Oberyn Martell, who saw the trial as a chance to avenge his sister's death. Oberyn got the admission he sought from Gregor Clegane during the trial by combat, but it came too late. Had Oberyn not overreached, he would have won Tyrion his freedom. Then again, had his opponent been anyone but Ser Gregor, it's difficult to see why Oberyn would defend Tyrion in the first place, just as it's hard to imagine Bronn taking up his cause had he not been a wealthy Lannister. In any case, Tyrion walked away from the Eyrie, innocence confirmed, but was consigned to the black cells of King's Landing, innocence be damned.

## In the Sight of Gods

Before demanding a trial by combat, Tyrion said, "The gods know the truth of my innocence. I will have their verdict, not the judgment of men." The choice between having a rational, evidence-based hearing and leaving one's fate to a higher, unseen power could not be more stark, though both reflect the influence that Westeros's predominant religion once had on the law. Until King Jaehaerys I put an end to it, the Faith had the power to hold trials and render punishments. Its sacred court comprised seven judges, one for each aspect of the religion. In much the same way, a "trial of seven" could be convened, whereby seven swordsmen lined up for the prosecution and seven for the defense. If one side was victorious over the other in battle, or even if one side failed to enlist seven swords, then the gods had made their ruling.

Queen Cersei restored the Faith's ability to try, as part of her scheme to bring about the downfall of her rival, Margaery Tyrell. Cersei planted evidence to implicate Margaery in acts of lewdness, fornication, adultery, and high treason. Women can't join the Night's Watch, so Margaery had fewer options than a common male criminal. Because she is a highborn lady of House Tyrell, however, she isn't destined to meet the King's Justice, at least not yet, and she has the right to a trial. Three of her seven judges would be female, representing the Maiden, the Mother, and the Crone. As the High Septon said, "Who could be more suited to judge the wickedness of women?" Ironically, Cersei faced the same options as Margaery after her schemes backfired badly. Ser Osney Kettleblack was meant to serve as a witness against Margaery, but the High Septon tortured him into exposing Cersei's sins, too. Cersei found herself accused of regicide, deicide, incest, and treason.

Both Cersei and Margaery suffered mightily while captives of the High Septon. He kept them isolated, fed them little, clothed them in nothing but roughspun shifts, and forbade them sleep. One of the attending septas explained, "Only the innocent know the peace of untroubled sleep. Confess your sins, and you will sleep like a newborn babe." That's about as comforting as telling an alleged witch, "If you cannot use magicks to save yourself from burning at the stake, then your agonizing death will have proven your innocence." Once again, we see the contradictions of Westerosi justice. The punishments that both women sustained here are their own kinds of trials, ones they could not escape without first confessing their guilt, true or not. And, once again, we see that a confession can free an accused from captivity, but not from further trials and punishments.

After admitting to a few of her transgressions, Cersei had to appeal to the citizens of King's Landing with a humble heart, shorn of secrets and concealments and literally naked before the eyes of gods and men, and she had to make a walk of atonement from the Great Sept of Baelor to the Red Keep. Although this punishment is cruel by any civilized standard, it's appropriate that Cersei didn't simply hold her head up high and endure it. She should have been humiliated because the entire act was humiliating – and also because she's guilty. (Of course, the walk of shame is a punishment reserved for women, much like taking the black is only for men. Otherwise, why wouldn't Tyrion and Eddard and so many others opt for the naked mile rather than risk losing their heads?)

The Seven aren't alone in intervening in mortal judgments. Beric Dondarrion captured Sandor Clegane and accused him of murder, adding, "It is not for us to judge you. Only the Lord of Light may do that now. I sentence you to trial by battle." Note the two irregularities here. First, Beric sentenced Sandor to a trial; sentencings usually follow the trials, not the other way around. Second, Clegane had already admitted to killing Arya's friend, the butcher's boy; a trial should have been unnecessary. All the same, Beric fought the Hound, and the Hound won. Apparently, the Lord of Light had judged him innocent because he was "not yet done" with him.

### The King's Justice, at Last?

It shouldn't be surprising that Westeros has no process for validating accusations, since it has no agencies for investigating crimes or identifying culprits, either. The limits of its ability to prosecute are exemplified by the three offices in the dungeons of King's Landing, one each for the chief gaoler, the lord confessor, and the King's Justice. Their responsibilities are, in order, to keep you in custody, wait for you to admit your crimes, and then execute your punishment. In other words, once caught, you are presumed guilty. If you're a commoner, you have little choice but to accept this. If you're highborn, you can hold out for a trial, but you may suffer more from your time in captivity than you would have with the usual punishment, and you may be forced to confess, anyway. Should you be granted a trial, you have two options: appear before the local lord or demand a trial by combat. In either case, you're subject to the unpredictable nature of the men who would judge or defend you. You may be condemned, even if you are innocent. You may walk free by the whimsy of the gods, even if you admit your guilt.

Clearly, trials give the illusion of justice, and nothing more. They are a spectacle, sometimes going so far as to sentence a woman to fight a bear. But trials – and the punishments they preface – keep the king's peace.  That is the primary difference between the king's justice and regular justice.  The former is more concerned with deterring further crimes and minimizing lawlessness; the latter has an interest in pursuing truth and punishing those who legitimately deserve it.

The two types of justices are not mutually exclusive.  Neither must they coexist.  Consider some outstanding cases:  Cersei faces another trial for the crimes she denies.  If she loses, will that discourage others from attempting regicide and deicide?  Or will it bring justice to the king and high septon she conspired to kill?  Doran Martell has long sought vengeance for the death of his sister, Elia.  He may shed enough blood to see justice done, but won't that necessarily disrupt the king's peace?  Bowen Marsh should be brought to justice for organizing a mutiny against Jon Snow.  The king's justice, however, may forgive Marsh, because he was looking out for the Watch and acted in the realm's best interests.

Predicting the outcomes of trials yet to come may be a fool's errand, but we shouldn't expect due process to prevail.  Westeros is ill-equipped to pursue anything but the king's justice, even if that means the innocent are sometimes punished and the guilty walk free.  The king's justice does not speak for truth or justice – such things are irrelevant to keeping the king's peace.  And the king's justice certainly isn't blind; it is as dependent on the man who stands accused as it is on the men who accuse, judge, and defend him.

Is that fair?  Just ask Ilyn Payne if the king's justice is fair, and see what he says.

# AFTERWORD

*Completed Songs and Frozen Conversations*

Now is the best time to be a *Song of Ice and Fire* fan. We are living in the Golden Age of this tale. The saga is unfinished, but that is exactly why this is the perfect time to be on board. When George R.R. Martin writes the final words and they are put to print, we will, most likely, have more answers than questions. But it is not the answers that make us strive to learn more. It is not the end that encourages us to continue on – it is the middle. It is the conflicts, and the questions, and the quest that make us yearn for more. Because we have to wait for an end is the reason a book like this one even exists. We are intrigued by what may happen and what we don't yet fully understand – and it is the reason why, when so many fans scream for George to hurry up and finish, I wonder, why the rush?

When I started reading *A Game of Thrones* over six years ago, I was lost in a dizzying haze of characters, castles, and cruelty. I liked it, but more details flew over my head than I care to admit. It wasn't until I joined the conversation online that I realized how deep this rabbit hole really went. R+L=J, secret Targs, Loras and Renly's relationship. How did I not see all this before?

Today, there are countless sites spawned by the success of HBO's *Game of Thrones*. All those years ago, however, I could find only three. Tower of the Hand became like a second home to me. I read essays, discussions, and theories. I would pick my book back up and flip to key moments and hidden gems, and everything just started to come together. It became this complex web of wonderful storytelling. It became more than just a novel I was reading – it became an experience, an event that I could share with others as it unfolded. If *A Song of Ice and Fire* had been finished when I first picked it up, I would have read and enjoyed it and been on to the next book, but it wasn't, and I had time to think and converse. I had time to learn what I had missed and think about what was to come. I had time to love it.

But, then again, I may be a bit biased. Talking about these books is my job. Okay – maybe not my job, since I don't get paid to podcast, but discussing theories like the ones here has literally changed my life. I've been introduced to more wonderful and interesting people than I can count. I've met and become friends with fellow fans and even actors from the show. I've been interviewed, televised, and put in print. I've even met and conversed with George himself on several occasions. And all this because I wanted to talk about a book that wasn't finished yet.

So join the conversation like I did. Read these theories and agree with them. Disagree with them. Hate them. Love them. Create your own. Just don't wait until the song is over and the discussion freezes. Do it now, while it still burns.

I guarantee you, it's one wild ride.


*Kyle Maddock*
*Co-host of A Podcast*
*of Ice and Fire*

# ABOUT THE AUTHORS

*Stefan Sasse* lives in Germany, where he teaches German literature, history, and political science. He started writing for Tower of the Hand in 2010 and continues to do so on a regular basis. He conducts the Boiled Leather Audio Hour podcast together with Sean T. Collins. In 2011, he wrote the re-read blog for *A Dance with Dragons*, located at adwd-reread.blogspot.com. You can read more of his work at his pop culture blog The Nerdstream Era: thenerdstreamera.blogspot.com.

@StefanSasse

*Miles Schneiderman* has read *A Song of Ice and Fire* so many times that he has completely lost touch with the difference between fantasy and reality. As a result, he asks for a maester when he gets sick and tries to send text messages by raven. For the past two years, he has been a semi-regular contributor of speculative analytical essays for Tower of the Hand, who is justified in not paying him by his belief that a "deadline" is something that happens to other people. Miles lives in Flagstaff, Arizona, where he studies journalism and political science at Northern Arizona University (a major in Westerosi history was, strangely, not available). When not doing schoolwork, he spends his time on the airwaves as a campus radio personality as well as reading, watching football, and plotting the demise of the global capitalist establishment. Don't say you weren't warned.

kjack.org

*Alexander Smith* is the co-creator of Tower of the Hand, responsible for crafting the chapter summaries and maintaining the Encyclopedia of Ice and Fire entries.

@towerofthehand

*Amin Javadi* is a co-founder of A Podcast of Ice and Fire, the longest-running podcast dedicated to George R.R. Martin's *A Song of Ice and Fire* saga. One of the two Canadians in the podcast crew, Amin started reading *Ice and Fire* in 2000, shortly before *A Storm of Swords* was released. He has guest-hosted on several *Ice and Fire* and *Game of Thrones* podcasts, including the Boiled Leather Audio Hour with Stefan Sasse and Sean T. Collins. He has founded several related podcasts, including the Bastards of Kingsgrave and the Vassals of Kingsgrave. Amin is a big fan of the FFG *Game of Thrones* board game adaptations, having played since the release of the first edition in 2003, and is a growing fan of the *Game of Thrones* card game. He can often be found debating rules and strategy with other online grand maesters. He can be reached via Tumblr at amin-j.

@JavadiAmin

*John T. Jasmin* is a computer programmer from Chicago, Illinois. After he read *A Game of Thrones* for the first time, he thought it would be neat to write a computer program that took an Excel spreadsheet that listed all of the books' characters and turn the data into family trees. He co-founded Tower of the Hand with Alex Smith shortly thereafter. Fun fact: John and George R.R. Martin lived in the same college dorm, albeit thirty years apart.

@jtjasmin

*Douglas Cohen* is a longtime fan of *A Song of Ice and Fire* and the proud owner of a signed first-edition hardcover of *A Game of Thrones*. He has appeared as a guest geek on *The Geek's Guide to the Galaxy* on Wired.com to discuss *A Dance with Dragons* with the co-hosts, and after each new episode of the HBO series, he feels compelled to write an extensive post on his personal blog. He is the former editor of *Realms of Fantasy* magazine, where he worked for six-and-a-half years. His fiction has appeared or is forthcoming in *Fantastic Stories of the Imagination, Space and Time, Interzone,* and *Weird Tales.* Along with John Joseph Adams, he is the co-editor of *Oz Reimagined: New Tales from the Emerald City and Beyond*, an original anthology from 47North, the new science fiction/fantasy publishing division of Amazon.com. To learn more, visit his blog: douglascohen.livejournal.com.

@Douglas_Cohen

*Marc N. Kleinhenz* has had some 300 articles published across 21 different sites, including IGN, *Orlando Attractions* magazine, Westeros.org, *The Escapist*, and, of course, Tower of the Hand, in addition to co-creating and co-hosting (for its first year) the Airship Travelogues podcast for Nintendojo.com. His creative writing has been published by Alterna Comics, MicroHorror.com, Death Head Grin, and *Asylum*

*Ink, Cuento*, and *Smashed Cat* magazines. His day jobs have ranged from everything from an intrepid GameStop employee to a *gaijin* English teacher in Japan to a mild-mannered medical supplies representative.

@msunyata

*Mimi Hoshut* was born in the Dothraki sea of Inner Mongolia and currently resides in Texas. Dubbed "Queen of the Podcasters" by George R.R. Martin, she founded A Podcast of Ice and Fire with Amin Javadi in 2008. When not postulating insane theories on the podcast, she attends graduate school for her master's in biotechnology, plays videogames with unwavering enthusiasm, and writes flash fiction on her blog.

mimihatesyou.com

Made in the USA
San Bernardino, CA
08 October 2013